CAN YOU
Hear Me
NOW?

CAN YOU
Hear Me
NOW?

Dallas and Nancy Demmitt

Foreword by Gary Smalley

Life Journey is an imprint of
Cook Communications Ministries, Colorado Springs, Colorado 80918
Cook Communications, Paris, Ontario
Kingsway Communications, Eastbourne, England

CAN YOU HEAR ME NOW?
© 2003 by Dallas and Nancy Demmitt. All rights reserved.

Printed in the United States of America

Unless otherwise indicated, all Scripture references are from *The Holy Bible: New International Version*®, NIV®. Copyright © 1973, 1978, 1984 by International Bible Society. Used by permission of Zondervan Publishing House. All rights reserved. Other references are taken from *The Message*. Copyright © by Eugene H. Peterson, 2002. Used by permission of NavPress Publishing Group; *The New Testament in Modern English* (PH), © 1965 by Washington, D.C., Canon Press (Christianity Today Version of *The New Testament in Four Versions*); and the *Amplified Bible*, (AMP)© 1965, the Lockman Foundation. Use by permission of Zondervan Publishing House. All rights reserved.

Edited by: Susan K. Goter
Senior Editor: Janet Lee
Cover and interior design by: Sandy Flewelling

Library of Congress Cataloging-in-Publication Data
Demmitt, Dallas.
   The gift of listening / Dallas and Nancy Demmitt; foreword by Gary Smalley.
      p. cm.
Includes bibliographical references.
   ISBN 0-7814-3896-9
   1. Listening--Religious aspects--Christianity. I. Demmitt, Nancy. II. Title.
   BV4647.L56 D46 2003
   248.8'4--dc21
                                    2002152147

contents

foreword

One day my wife and I were planning to leave for a camping trip, which we had discovered was a way to spend quality time together. I got up early to jog, and while I was running I had what I thought was a great idea—I wanted to do something special and unexpected for Norma, just to show her some love and honor. I knew she liked to have breakfast with her friend, Helen, so I decided I'd encourage her to have breakfast out with her friend while I packed the camper. Then when she got home she could simply slide into the front seat and—voila!—we would embark on our journey in the wilderness. I thought she would be delighted to have a leisurely breakfast with Helen instead of slaving over the camper and the accompanying hassles of leaving.

"I've got a surprise for you" I sang to Norma that morning.

She eyed me warily from behind her coffee cup.

"What's that?" she asked.

"I want you to go to breakfast with Helen while I pack the camper. Then, when you get back from breakfast, the camper will be ready and we can go!"

Well, she didn't think much of my idea at all. Instead, she bristled.

"Gary, you know that I always need to pack for myself," she said.

Being a woman of precise detail and order, Norma interpreted my offer as a "ploy" to get her out of my way so that I could pack the camper the way I wanted to. Of course, that was not my intention at all; I honestly had no secret motive. That she thought my innocent offer was some sort of scheme made me angry. I wanted to scream, "Okay, then, you pack the camper, and I'll go enjoy breakfast with Helen!"

Norma's suspicion had invalidated my loving offer and got our supposedly blissful camping trip off to a rocky start.

Now, let's replay the scene using listening skills in this important book from Dallas and Nancy Demmitt. Instead of hurting my feelings with her negative interpretations, Norma could have used the listening in this book to establish my intentions.

I would've rushed into the kitchen, shouting, "I've got a surprise for you!" and then tell her my idea about her breakfasting with Helen while I packed the camper.

She could have taken time to *listen* to what I was saying and, instead of accusing me, she could have tried to understand me—by repeating what she'd thought she'd heard me say.

"Let me see if I'm hearing you correctly," she would have said, "You're saying you want to pack the camper. And you want me to go to breakfast with Helen. Then when I get back, it will all be done?"

"Yes, exactly!" I would have confirmed. "Tell me how you like that."

By asking her to tell me how she liked the idea in a non-threatening, non-accusatory way, I would have initiated the gift of listening. At this point, if she still had suspicions of ulterior motives, she could have employed additional listening techniques to ferret out the truth. "But are you really saying that you want me to get out of here so you can pack the camper the way you like it?" she could have said.

At that point, I could have told Norma that she had gotten wrong information.

"I'm feeling that you're only trying to get me out of the house so you can pack the camper any way you want," she would have said. But I wouldn't react to that line out of insecurity; I'd merely explain my true intention.

"No, that is not what I meant at all," I could have said. "I just wanted to make your life easier and give you the morning off."

If escalation begins, just take a time out and tell each other that you will revisit this issue later after you have both had a chance to calm down. When you meet to discuss the issue again, using the listening methods in this book, you'll be amazed at your increased calm.

But, of course, Norma and I didn't know any of this on the morning of our camping trip. So we hastily packed our camper together in silence. Then, nursing our separate emotional wounds, we drove off toward our campsite, abandoning the search for intimacy and speaking instead in cold clichés and empty facts.

Listening can help you avoid misunderstanding and conflict, reduce false assumptions, stop the natural tendency to react in the panic or crisis mode, and reduce fear, loneliness, and pain. As the Demmitts write: "Just showing someone that you are willing to listen—without condemning or judging them—will help to make that person feel valued, loved, honored, and appreciated."

To learn the power of listening, you'll have to begin with one vow: to rid yourself of what the Demmitts call the "How-can-I-get-you-to-shut-up-and-listen-to-me?" mind-set and replace it with a "What-can-I-do-to-create-a-safe-place-where-understanding-can-take-root-and-grow?" attitude. In the pages of this book, you will learn from Dallas and Nancy how to improve and master one of the most critical communications skills in every day life—listening.

I want to encourage you to turn the pages of this book in a slow and thoughtful manner. Sit down and get comfortable and prepare to learn some fascinating information, which if continually practiced, will change your life forever. Open your heart and prepare yourself to experience the power of listening.

Gary Smalley, Branson, Missouri

acknowledgments

Our thanks to Gary Smalley whose infectious enthusiasm for our work and willingness to recommend us in the publishing world got us started on this journey.

To Bill McCartney who challenged us to get our "stuff" in writing and has been open to being coached in giving the gift of listening.

To Terry Whalin from Cook Communications Ministries who believed in us and in this book and to the Cook publishing staff for their patience and persistence in putting up with our naiveté and for encouraging us when we despaired.

To Steve McVey who blessed us both with his encouragement to write this book, and with the abundance of live-changing information we soaked up from his ministry. We are continually fed and blessed by his books and tapes.

To Bobby Capps who took the concepts in this book, and ran with them. He called us every other day with another new story of how God had used the concepts in his life and ministry. His excitement and energy sparked us on when the going was tough, and who has allowed the Holy Spirit to expand and multiply what he heard from us many times over. His stories appear throughout this book.

To Ray Vialpando who has long embraced these concepts and whose friendship, encouragement and ability to communicate the love of God continually nurture us and spur us on.

To Tom and Marilyn Burger for their friendship and encouragement and for their involvement and leadership in taking this ministry to a larger audience.

To our "Marriage by Grace" class at Word of Grace and to our Senior Minister, Gary Kinnaman who has enriched and encouraged us.

To the men's groups Dallas has attended during the past fifteen years and all the men who have contributed by sharing their lives with him. Bill Lawrence, Bob Hamilton, Scott Malm, Paul Hauber, Ray Jensen, and Joe Renaldo are some of those men.

And to all those who faithfully listened to our hearts and prayed for us as this book progressed.

And I (Dallas) want to acknowledge my mother and grandmother who always had time to listen while I was growing-up.

Most of all we thank the Lord Jesus. May he be glorified and may his love and healing-presence be revealed to every person who reads this book.

Dedication

To Beth and Lori, who served as "guinea pigs" as we learned to apply these concepts at home and who now allow the Lord to use them to give the gift of listening.

introduction

The Importance of Communication

For the past thirty years we have worked individually and together as Christian counselors. Throughout many of those years, we've helped people with their underlying primary need—communication.

When we began specializing in teaching communication skills in a large group counseling practice in Scottsdale, Arizona, our colleagues and our clients were enthusiastic. Couples seemed to improve almost immediately. And our own relationship thrived as we applied the techniques we taught to hundreds of couples.

Clearly communication was the key to successful marriage. Yet as the years passed, we noticed that many couples couldn't sustain these communication changes in their marriages. Some couples returned to counseling feeling discouraged and defeated. Or worse, we would hear about their divorces. Even in our own marriage, as time and life's pressures increased, we discovered that we couldn't consistently practice what we had spent years teaching to others. Despite the time we spent teaching and practicing effective communication, we lashed out at each other with increasing frequency. Our own failures both embarrassed and confused us.

On one occasion in utter frustration, I (Nancy) picked up the communication manual we used in our seminars and threw it across our bedroom in my husband's direction, yelling, "These communication skills simply do not work!"

Now Dallas and I know it wasn't the communication skills that didn't work. Something inside us rendered us unable to "work" the skills. It was years before we discovered the missing ingredient.

As we recognized our own need to improve our communication, we discovered mere skills, training, or behavior modification techniques were not enough for sustained change. Techniques would bring temporary improvement and generate some excitement and hope, but they were powerless to produce lasting change.

Thankfully, our search for answers sent us to draw upon our faith in God. And through the years we began to see that human beings—ourselves included—need a mind-change before the heart-change and behavior-change can occur.

Ultimately, in the lab of our counseling practice and our own marriage, God showed us the liberating truths about the gift of listening that are contained in this book. These truths have brought a consistent flow of peace and love into our lives, as well as the lives of people whom we coach. As we've offered the gift of listening to those around us, both friends and strangers, we've seen God work in astounding ways.

Once you start thinking seriously about your own communication skills as they are woven into your personal faith in Christ, you'll see what can happen when you offer this valuable gift to others.

Dallas and Nancy Demmitt
Summer 2002

1

The Broken Bridge

*Without good communication, a relationship is merely a
hollow vessel carrying you along on a frustrating journey fraught
with the perils of confusion, projection, and misunderstanding.*
Cherie Carter-Scott

Kim tingled with anticipation. She wanted to surprise her
husband, Don, to mark his fortieth birthday with an over-the-hill
party.

Two blocks from his office, Kim called his secretary on her cell
phone and asked, "Has he gone to lunch yet? I want to check his
e-mail addresses for business associates and friends to invite to the
party."

"The coast is clear," his secretary said. "He won't be back for at
least an hour."

They chatted briefly, laughing about the one-foot-in-the-grave
party theme with black crepe paper and balloons.

"He won't ever forget this birthday," she said, not realizing the significance of these words.

Kim parked and a few moments later opened the door of Don's office. As she breathed, she caught the fresh wood scent of his cologne, which still clung to the air.

Pausing a moment, she looked at the picture of the two of them on his desk, smiling into each other's eyes. How she loved this handsome, strong, successful man. God had blessed them with two beautiful children and a lovely old home, which they were restoring. And she was blessed with a husband who still made her toes curl, just as much now as in the early days of their relationship. She glanced at her watch and knew she had to hurry before he returned.

Quickly she approached the computer and, with one stroke of a finger, her birthday anticipation turned into shock and horror. Her life would never be the same.

On his screen, she read these words:

Happy Birthday Darling. Can't wait to see you again.
Love, Claudia

The confusing jumble of words seemed to float there, just below the email addresses. *This must be a joke*, she assumed. *One of his friends is just teasing as a birthday prank.* But as Kim scrolled through Don's inbox, the same address appeared over and over again: *claudia@internet.com*. Then she read more of the messages and saw they were personal and shameless. The words told the story of an intimate relationship. These messages ripped apart the illusion of her safe world and her Christian marriage. Barely able to control her shaking as she slipped on her dark glasses, Kim walked toward the car and used her cell phone to dial her pastor.

Three months later Kim called our office at her pastor's urging. The divorce would be final in six weeks, yet she agreed to some counseling sessions with us because she didn't want anyone saying she had not tried everything to save her marriage. She announced to us, "I'll give it these last six weeks but not a minute longer."

Nothing could change Kim's resolve—not even Don's tearful repentance or the pleading of her pastor. Kim felt her husband had ruined her life. Like a strategically placed bomb exploding with maximum impact, the scandal rocked the local church family. Don resigned from the church board, which was at the same church Claudia and her family attended. After Don's resignation, Claudia and her husband stepped down from leadership in the youth group. The children of both families, ages ten to nineteen, had been close friends, and their relationships reverberated with the aftershock. The scandal continued to ricochet and impact the young people who admired both couples.

After Claudia's husband filed for divorce, neither family appeared in the church. It was too painful for these family members to face everyone. The children's eyes radiated shock, shame, and disbelief. The stable and familiar relationships that comprised the rich fabric of the church family were also severed.

For church damage control, the leadership called a special meeting. Young people asked their parents difficult questions that reflected their loss of idealism. Teenagers wondered: *Is Christian marriage a bad joke? Does Christ really make a difference in people's lives? If these two families of good church people fractured and tore, how can we hope to have long-lasting marriages?*

During our over thirty years of marriage counseling, we've seen hundreds of individuals—but no two people in a more dismal marriage situation. Our prayer for them was like every person who comes to us for help: *Lord, open their eyes to see how capable they are in you. Only your presence can make a difference here.*

Today, three years later, Kim and Don still live in the house that they were remodeling at the time of Don's fortieth birthday. Now the house is a finished project and full of gleaming, polished wood floors and antiques made more valuable because the couple found them together. In some ways their home is like their marriage—glowing with the warmth of love and hard work they have invested into it.

Their older children are gone, securely launched into productive, faith-filled lives. And Kim and Don radiate a type of humility and gentleness that wasn't present in their lives three years earlier. If someone asks them about that dark time, they smile and mention the grace of God.

Before we detail what changed Kim and Don's situation, let's consider another family in crisis. The same skills and principles that helped Kim and Don rebuild also assisted these troubled parents reconnect with Jason, their rebellious sixteen-year-old son.

"First of all, we want you to know that we love our son," said Susan, glancing at her son slouched on a chair in the corner. After a long history of family problems, the three of them had come for to us for help. "We have done our best to teach him Christian principles," Susan said. "He knows the Bible, and he's been in church almost every week since he was two weeks old. We can't imagine what's gotten into him." She dabbed her eyes with a damp tissue wadded in her hand.

"For three years he has given us nothing but grief," said Bob, his father. "He's run with the wrong crowd ... been kicked out of school ... and recently the police picked him up for shoplifting."

After several more minutes of that truthful, but painful review of their son's misbehavior, I (Dallas) turned to the teen and said, "Jason, I'd like to hear from you about what's happening."

Before Jason could answer, his father barked, "Sit up, Jason. Show a little respect!"

Jason came alive, eyes narrow, body coiled like a steel spring. "Get off my case! I'll sit like I want to!"

"You will not speak to me that way!" Bob yelled, jumping to his feet.

"I'll speak to you any way I want to!" the son yelled back, rising out of his chair.

Bob and Susan raised Jason on the standard of God's Word, but they came to us feeling heartsick and confused. What can a father do when his son becomes the enemy and rises up to challenge his authority in the home? Their teenager was unable to receive their love in the way they had packaged it, yet he desperately needed their support and encouragement. He felt deeply discouraged and alone.

Thankfully, much has happened since that exchange in our office. The changes in Jason and his parents were not an overnight miracle, but in time the family learned how to listen and to see each other in a whole new way. This process was initiated when Susan and Bob learned how to see and hear the real Jason.

The same results and principles that Jason and his parents discovered also enabled Meg to resolve issues with her roommates. Meg had moved out of her college dorm into an apartment with two of her Christian friends, Julie and Karen. Together they managed the rent, so the trio signed a six-month lease. At first the freedom and independence was exciting—but the excitement soon wore off. Meg was shocked that Karen and Julie had boys in the apartment at all hours. And much to her surprise and frustration, both of her roommates seemed oblivious to sharing the chores. Unless Meg cleaned things up, the apartment stayed in a constant mess.

"I've tried to talk to them about it," Meg said, "but they don't seem to be listening. Lately they treat me like I'm the enemy or the housemother or something. And I'm beginning to feel like I'm the only grownup around. My grades are suffering. I'm not getting enough sleep. What's the Christian thing to do?"

Today as she reflects on this experience, Meg says, "That six months was more valuable than many of the classes I attended in four years of college." What did she learn? She learned how to speak up with confidence and clarity in a tough situation. Also she learned how to calmly, respectfully, and firmly express her point of view and how to invite the others to do the same.

"But most of all," she says, "I found out who I really am. Before, I tried so hard to please everyone. I guess I thought if they liked me, I must be okay. Now I love me, warts and all."

The relationship challenges in the stories above have different roots, but the situations were all resolved using the same principles.

Their relationship knots untangled when they learned to draw on hidden resources they didn't know they possessed. These resources equipped them to pick up the broken fragments of their relationships and put them together again in a fresh, new way. Each person experienced significant, lasting changes by applying biblical principles and communication skills that you can apply to your life as well.

In the following chapters, you will learn about a powerful combination of truth and skill development to change yourself and your relationships. These truths can liberate and empower you far beyond your imagination, and the skills will enable you to translate truth into action.

Can You Hear Me Now? will teach you skills to enable you to speak and listen at a deeper level of communication. This book will enable you to:

Venture boldly past the surface to the deeper matters of the heart;

Uncover the hidden motivations that cause conflict; and

Heal and resolve longstanding issues in your relationships.

Through this material you will learn how to stop reacting to the situations that used to trigger your defenses. Also you will learn how to listen and speak with skill, confidence, and respect.

The practical portion of the book is divided into two skill sets: *Discovery Listening* and *Discovery Talking*.

Discovery listening skills can take you beyond what you thought you knew about listening into new realms of personal and relationship discovery. *Discovery talking skills* are designed to help you better understand your own heart—and to express your heart to others.

The two sets of skills that you will learn are like two mighty pillars under a bridge built on the bedrock of who you are in Christ. He's the Rock. Everything else is built on Him. *Anchoring* is the act of trusting in His presence to undergird and animate the communication process and will be explained in detail in chapter 3.

Building Bridges Through Communication

Let's face it, the majority of our struggles in life—whether in relationship with God, a spouse, a friend, or a colleague—center on a breakdown in communication. Unfortunately, many people have a wrong concept about the keys to communication.

The majority of people treat the process of communication like an airplane ride. They have a place they want to take us and they want to get us there *quickly*. Other people see communication as a subway, which has a preplanned route, unmovable guidelines, and a hidden agenda beneath the surface. In reality, good communication is more like a bridge. Consider two people standing on opposite sides of a large canyon without a bridge to connect them. They have no way to reach one another—no way to communicate or collaborate or touch each other's lives. Now insert a bridge between them. With the bridge in place, each person can walk across to see the world from a different perspective. They can travel freely back and forth to broaden their viewpoint and enrich their experience. Now they can pool resources and unite around common goals.

But not just any bridge will do. People need a bridge they can trust—a strong, safe structure that will support them and the ones they love in good times and bad. When you think of a strong bridge, what picture comes to your mind? We think of the bridges we see along the interstate in Arizona. Across the desert, there are bridges over dry riverbeds—rivers with names, but without a single drop of water in their banks.

To many people, these bridges would appear to be a ridiculous waste of taxpayers' money. Yet during the rainy season, these empty washes will become filled with flash flood rivers that will flow with devastating force. It is essential that each of these bridges be built upon a strong foundation—with huge concrete pillars. Just as these physical bridges require a strong foundation to stand against the rush of a raging river, you need a strong, safe structure beneath you to weather the relationship storms in your life. You need a bridge that is anchored on bedrock—solid, secure, enduring whatever life brings your way.

We believe that each of the huge supporting pillars resting on bedrock is the truth that God desires to anchor your life to the solid foundation of His love. He has already secured your life with His presence, living on the inside the moment you received His Son. The bridge that connects you with another person represents the communication skills (discovery listening and discovery talking), undergirded by God's presence. When you cross the bridge that spans the chasm between you and another, you are trusting that God will secure you and animate your words. He is your confidence. He supplies all that you need—love, wisdom, patience, and peace—all that is required as you give the gift of listening.

Crossing a bridge without Jesus animating and energizing it is like running over a rickety footbridge, with slats falling into the chasm below and bad guys following in hot pursuit. Communication without dependence on the indwelling Christ is unsafe and unwise.

The skills we offer are powerful, relationship-healing tools when placed in God's hand. Imagine a large hand from God invisibly holding up the bridge. God is the hand securing the communication process. You provide the unique personality and the packaging through which the life of God moves. He provides, through His grace, everything else.

The gift of listening examines communication—those practical, easy-to-understand listening and speaking skills that equip you to establish loving, fulfilling, healthy relationships. As you understand the details of the gift of listening, you also increase your understanding of the ultimate gift of God's grace—Christ in you (Colossians 1:27).

Through God's grace, you will recognize that you have far more to offer in your relationships than you may realize.

Earlier in this chapter you met people who were at different places on the road to relationship disaster. Instead of becoming communication casualties, each person wisely reached out for assistance. Their search began in a counseling office and ended in a seminar that provided additional information and practical experience. As they applied the principles, they achieved positive changes in their lives. You also can discover these principles as you work through this book.

Now, let's get started!

Questions for Personal Reflection or Group Discussion:

- *Take a moment and reflect on the stories in chapter 1. What relationship or situation comes to mind when you think about your own life?*

- *If you could choose one thing you would like the Lord to accomplish in your life as you apply what you learn in this book, what would it be?*

2

The Cry of the Heart: Nobody's Listening

*The feeling of not being understood is one
of the most painful in human experience.*
Michael Nichols[1]

Do you have a teenager in your home? If so, the following conversation between an inquisitive dad and his tight-lipped sixteen-year-old son might seem familiar:

> Dad: *"So what's going on in your world these days, son?"*
> Son: *"Nothing much."*
> Dad: *"How's school?"*
> Son: *"Fine."*
> Dad: *"Well, what are you learning?"*
> Son: *"Stuff."*
> Dad: *"Anything you want to tell me about?"*
> Son: *"Nope."*

For many parents, that strained exchange is all too common. Bombarded with questions from a parent, the teen doesn't want to open up. The lack of significant conversation between moody teens and their anxious elders is often a major challenge during some tough adolescent years. Adults find themselves cut off at a time when they long to know what's going on in their teen's mind. But they shut down as if preoccupied with packing their bags to leave home, leaving the parent feeling discarded and unnecessary. Giving the gift of listening keeps the shell open. The teens receive the encouragement and respect they need, and the adult may get to tuck in some last-minute, well-timed, and strategically placed pearls of wisdom.

Before we discover how to give the gift of listening, let's leave The Clam and his dad with their particular challenges and check in on another set of communicators. Possibly in recent days you've heard a conversation similar to the following one at your house.

Meet Ted and Donna, who are talking in the kitchen after dinner, while their children pour over their homework in the adjoining room.

Donna: "You never talk to me."

Ted: "What do you mean, I never talk to you? I'm talking to you now."

Donna: "But we never talk about things that matter."

Ted: "What do you mean, 'things that matter'? What do you want to talk about?"

Donna: "Oh, I don't know. Anything. Like what you are feeling."

Ted: "Well, right now I'm feeling that you're bugging me."

Donna: "… Bugging you! Forget it! I can't talk to you."

Ted: "What do you mean, you can't talk to me? For Pete's sake … What do you want to say?"

Whether you are a Ted or a Donna, few couples deny that when it comes to communication, men and women are often at cross purposes. Both members feel alone, confused, and frustrated with their relational blockages. The woman wants to communicate about feelings and to be connected to her mate on an emotional

level. The man wants to communicate on a logical, rational level.
Finally, because neither one of them makes sense to the other, their
attempts to communicate may cease altogether. The relationship
begins to feel more like a punishment than their hopes and dreams
for a satisfying, peaceful union.

Our communication challenges are not only in family relationships. Here's another situation, which you may have experienced:

Sam runs a large corporation on the East Coast and has one of
his managers, John, drop into his office to discuss a problem.

John: *I'm struggling to know how to help Brenda. Several times a
week she arrives late to work. We've talked about it but I never
get any straight answers.*

Sam *(looking impatient):* *Here's what you do, John. You keep track
of these late arrivals, write them up, and turn them into Human
Resources. Let the HR people take care of it. It's one of their
functions, and you can then press on to other more important
things.*

Typical for many people, Sam doesn't listen to John but jumps
into the conversation fray with a solution and a "fix." Instead of
exploring some of the possible reasons and approaches John could
use to learn about Brenda's lateness, Sam provides the fix. Through
Sam's fix, John will soon be faced with another set of problems—
looking for another competent employee to replace Brenda—
instead of keeping Brenda as a productive member of the team.
Instead of lowering John's stress and helping him explore options
through listening, Sam is adding to John's stress and stack of problems. Both men have mutual goals and tasks to complete. But
because Sam doesn't listen, John is locked into his own agenda and
is a million miles apart from Sam. The missing element is mutual
respect, which contains two elements: a heart-change and a head-
change. The heart-change involves a whole new look at reality—
who you are and what's possible for your life and your relationships.
The head-change involves skill development—a new way of listening and talking, a bridge to teamwork and mutual respect.

New Insight on Listening

Possibly you've had some listening training in the past. This book is more than the common "active listening" techniques. We believe there are at least four levels of listening.

1. No Listening or Nonlistening: This person has no awareness of the need to listen or to use a set of skills related to listening. He is not hearing impaired, so he believes he is a listener.

2. Focused Listening: This listening is the type you do in polite conversation. The listener looks at the speaker with interest and doesn't interrupt him. Most people prefer to speak, so focused listening is greatly valued and appreciated.

3. Active Listening: This type of listener will paraphrase or summarize what the other person is speaking and it helps the speaker feel more deeply connected. This type of listening fosters trust, communicates caring, and invites open dialogue. Also it can clarify miscommunication and resolve conflict.

4. Discovery Listening: This level encompasses the first three levels, but moves the listener to a whole new dimension of listening. This skill set is life changing, and God is clearly active in this type of listener. As the other person opens his heart, the listener helps in a deeper way than ever before. Chapter 5 will explain this concept in depth.

Like the people in these scenarios, our whole culture cries out, "Won't someone please listen to me? Won't anyone acknowledge my presence and the importance of my feelings and experiences?"

We Are in a Listening Crisis

People long to be heard, but few people know how to listen. Individuals don't know how to tune in to each other, or to their children, or even to their own hearts. And yet, how can someone expect to listen when nobody has heard *his* needs and experiences?

When people are not heard or understood, they don't feel valued. When they don't feel valued, self-esteem suffers. With time, low self-esteem "paralyzes our potential, destroys our dream, ruins our relationships, and sabotages our Christian service," notes author David Seamands in *Healing of Memories*.[2]

Another result of our high-tech, low-touch, listening-deprived culture is loneliness. People have increased the amount of their communication, but they enjoy it less! We are in the information age—our lives are bombarded every day by the radio, the television, the newspaper, magazines, and the Internet. Yet increased information has only increased the need for listening.

Each of us is awash in insignificant communication, which leaves us exhausted at the end of the day. The information super-highway whirls around us at dizzying speeds. Chat rooms buzz with interaction. Participants juggle three and four conversations while instant messaging each other over the Internet, volleying back and forth short messages to represent the complexity of their lives. Yet, we still feel lonely.

On the Internet, people reveal their souls to faceless strangers through anonymous and sometimes desperate dialogues that occur at breakneck speeds. In cyberspace, people will take communications risks to try to ease the loneliness, while searching for answers. Despite these conveniences, our communication frenzy is still marked with an absence of caring, purposeful, loving listening.

We Participate in Verbal Ping-Pong

We're exposed to millions of words thrown out there for us to absorb, yet we often feel we haven't had a significant communication all day. We absorb so much that is not satisfying without realizing it and wonder why we feel glutted and yet empty at the end of a day. We've feasted on verbal Twinkies, but we're longing for a nutritious meal!

Communication is taking place, but usually the interaction takes the form of ping-pong. It's the shallow exchange and the superficial conversation where people are "talking" but connecting very little on a heart or feeling level. Everyone's expressing and reacting—and nobody's listening.

We are all familiar with the term "hearing impaired" as a disability afflicting individuals. But what about those who are "listening impaired?" Isn't this a relational disability?

Likewise in the church, everyone can name an abundance of gifted "talkers"—the preachers, teachers, exhorters, prophets, and discerners. *But where are the gifted listeners?*

When we ask people in our seminars which role they prefer— talking or listening—only a few prefer listening. Perhaps it is because we prefer the role that draws attention to ourselves. Why do we love the limelight and avoid being the audience, the ones who make the talking role possible? Isn't it ironic that *speech* is usually a required subject in high school? Where is the instruction in *listening*? Good listening is far more difficult than talking—so difficult and selfless that it requires the indwelling Christ in order to do it effectively.

Listening as a Gift

James reminds us in Scripture that "… every good and perfect gift comes from God" (James 1:17). Then he challenges us, "Be quick to listen, slow to speak, and slow to become angry, for man's anger does not bring about the righteous life that God desires" (James 1:19). Most of us understand and are familiar with the type of anger that results when someone is not heard. It's a challenge to practice the admonition for quick listening. So, let's learn how to be *quick to listen.*

Solomon prayed for this ability. Specifically, he prayed for wisdom. The *Amplified Bible* translates the word "wisdom" as "… an understanding mind and a hearing heart," (1 Kings 3:9, AMP). These two components, an understanding mind and a hearing heart, comprise the best definition we've seen that describes the perfect kind of listening.

How do you get this "listening" kind of wisdom? James again provides an answer. He said, "If any man lacks wisdom, let him ask of God," (1:5, NKJV).

The Apostle Paul warned against boasting about our own wisdom. He then said two life-changing things: "... you are in Christ Jesus, who has become for us wisdom from God—that is, our righteousness, holiness and redemption"(1 Cor. 1:30), and "... we have the mind of Christ" (1 Cor. 2:16).

What a relief to know that when we have Jesus, we have His mind that contains the wisdom of God! In fact, when we have Christ, we get it all—His mind, His righteousness, and all the rest of Him—including His ability to listen with an understanding mind and a hearing heart.

Why Listening Is Important

Gifted listening opens powerful pathways for intimate, vulnerable, satisfying relationships. Through this kind of listening, God gifts us to move forward together in mutually satisfying, productive teamwork to carry out His command to love one another and share that love with the world around us.

Listening clears and prevents misunderstanding

Everyone has had the unhappy experience of someone else explaining our words, when their interpretation couldn't be further from the truth. The Bible shares some terse words on this topic: "To answer before listening is both stupid and rude" (Prov. 18:13, *The Message*).

Isn't it natural to assume you know what someone else is saying? In a couple of eye blinks, we quickly respond while being totally unaware that *we answered before we listened*. When we answer before listening, we prove to others that we are both *stupid* and *rude*.

Listening helps you focus on understanding what the speaker is saying, clarify each building block of the message as you receive it,

and make sure the message you hear is the intended message from
the speaker.

Listening helps prevent emotional reacting

Effective listening can help you move away from turbulent
emotional storms and into the calmer waters of reason. Emotional
and rational thinking are powerful components of who you are and
how you express yourself. Both components are essential to good
communication. When you enter the choppy waters of negative
emotions—such as fear, anger, hurt, or guilt—the dialogue can
degenerate quickly into an out-of-control emotional hurricane.

However, when you respond as an effective listener and use the
skills presented in the following chapters, much emotional
whiplash can be eliminated. Listening provides a rational, logical,
more structured way to respond. As you operate in a more structured form, it tends to stimulate left-brain activity and bring the
exchange into balance. As a result, you can talk about stormy issues
within the calm, rational structure of listening.

Listening can build or rebuild trust

Each of us knows what it feels like when a trusted relationship
is violated. It hurts when someone you love, or want to love, treats
you with disrespect. A lack of listening in a relationship is both
disrespectful and hurtful. When you are continually misunderstood,
and you can no longer communicate with each other because anger
and fear have built up, your relationship no longer feels safe.

Listening helps you rebuild safety and trust into your relationship. The gift of listening provides a structure for trust to grow and
flourish.

Listening helps you make personal discoveries

Listening clears the confusion and allows you to answer the
searching questions of life such as: *What's going on with me? Why
does this hurt so much? What is God trying to tell me? Where am I
going, and how am I going to get there?*

Many of us have solutions to our own problems. Years of answers are tucked away in our brains from a variety of educational experiences such as sermons, memory verses, schooling, books, and life experience. This wealth of information is stored inside—like buried treasure waiting to be found.

While you may have a mental file cabinet of answers for your choices, you may not have good listeners to help you find this internal treasure. To locate this treasure, you must sift through the confusion of emotions and half-baked ideas that float around in your mind. We call this sorting process *going for the gold*.

When you invite Jesus Christ, the Wonderful Counselor, to orchestrate going for the gold, it is not just a matter of listening. It's a sacred, spiritual journey into the soul of another human being. Jesus is in charge; you don't have to force a "discovery" to happen. As listeners, we've witnessed many times the dynamic change that takes place in the lives of individuals. When you are the listener, you receive the privilege of witnessing God at work. You are the instrument, and He is the life-changer.

Listening helps you make high-quality joint decisions

A consistent theme throughout the Bible is the importance of unity among believers. From the smallest unit—a Christian couple, roommates, or friends—to the global Christian community, a crying need exists for Christians to understand each other. Often we long to discover the mutual "mind of Christ," then move forward together in faith and unity. Listening helps you discover the mind of Christ for dreams and goals you share with others.

Learning to Use the Gift of Listening

In the first chapter, we introduced the gift of listening as a two-part communication process that empowers and enables you to improve your communication with others. The two skill sets that make up the gift of listening are as follows:

Discovery Listening is participating in an individual's discovery and resolution of personal or relationship issues through the use of gifted listening.

Discovery Talking is the discovery and resolution of personal or relationship issues, with or without the aid of a gifted listener.

When God created the earth, He declared each day that all of His creation was good. The first "not good" thing noted in Genesis wasn't Adam's sin, but rather Adam's "aloneness". Consider this for a moment: Adam had everything a man could possibly want—an intimate relationship with God, an exalted position as CEO of a beautiful animal and garden empire. And yet God declared his aloneness wasn't good. Mankind wasn't created to live in isolation.

Yet even in marriage, a high percentage of people report feeling alone and lonely. Likewise many church members, roommates, children, pastors—people in all kinds of relationships—report loneliness and isolation as the dominating emotional landscape of their lives.

So how does the gift of listening eliminate or alleviate loneliness? As you complete the chapters in this book, you'll see this process provides a bridge to connect people at the heart level in ways that untangle relationship knots and invite intimate, vulnerable, satisfying relationships.

If you are helping a friend, a child, your spouse, or a business relationship, you'll discover how the gift of listening offers simple tools that God can use in profound ways. Because God does the work, you don't have to carry the load or experience the compassion fatigue that often comes when we try to change others.

The gift of listening can impact your life in many ways. One important benefit you'll experience is profound relief from the exhaustion of trying in vain to untangle your relationship knots. Have you ever tried to untangle fishing line? Last summer, we took our grandsons fishing. In a few short hours, three active boys—ages six, nine, and eleven—produced two small fish, two exhausted grandparents, and hopelessly tangled fishing lines. After that long day, we found it easier to throw away the tangled fishing line than attempt to unravel the knots.

Have you felt the same way about some of your relationship knots? Maybe in your experience, it's easier to discard relationships rather than untangle them.

A woman had many gold chains hanging on a jewelry tree on her dresser. Somehow, these chains became a complex tangle in a messy clump. Despite her effort and a patient attempt from her husband to untangle them, she could not separate any of the chains. While each one had worth and sentimental value, the woman threw away the valuable gold chains.

In many ways, we mirror those tangled gold chains. Sometimes we *won't, can't,* or *don't know how* to do the hard work of untangling our relational knots. We choose to discard the relationship, despite our recognition that this relationship has significant value.

The gift of listening offers relief from the exhaustion and hopelessness you feel when your relationship knots become more hopelessly entangled. The longer you work on the relationship, the more tangled the knots. Through the gift of listening, you can untangle the knots and preserve these precious God-given relationships.

Questions for Personal Reflection or Group Discussion:

- *As you consider this list of benefits from effective listening, which ones mean the most to you and why?*
  - ☐ *Clears and prevents misunderstanding*
  - ☐ *Prevents emotional reacting*
  - ☐ *Builds or rebuilds trust*
  - ☐ *Helps you find solutions and make discoveries for your life*
  - ☐ *Helps you make high-quality joint decisions*

- *If you have not already done so, identify a particular relationship "knot" you would like the Lord to untangle as you apply the concepts in this book.*

3

Why Listening Is So Hard

Conversation: *A vocal competition in which the one who is catching his breath is called the listener.*
Anonymous

Because you are continuing to read this book on listening, we assume you want to drop out of this type of competition! Or perhaps a well-intentioned friend or family member has given you this book to challenge you to catch your breath! No matter whether you *want* to learn or *need* to learn more about this topic, let's establish a foundational truth: *Listening is hard work.*

Listening is the essence of patient and unselfish communication. It requires you to put aside your own issues—and your clamoring thoughts, needs, and emotions—in order to hear someone else. It means working to understand someone else's point of view, even when you don't agree with his perspective.

Listening requires holding yourself in neutral long enough to thoroughly understand another person without offering a fix or a solution to his problem, nor offering an opposing point of view. The act of listening is a demonstration of what the Bible calls "dying to self." When it comes to communication, the acid test for understanding how "dead" you are is in how well you *listen*, not how well you *talk*.

The Problem

Communication in Christian circles far too often resembles communication in the world in general where speaker and listener are constantly switching roles, both jockeying for position; one's needs competing with the other's. If you don't believe it, try telling another Christian about a problem you're having and see how long it takes for this person to interrupt you to tell you about a problem of his own, or to offer advice—advice you may have already considered, or that may suit him more than it does you.

The following story comes from a friend, Tim, who was looking for a "hearing heart and an understanding mind" in a small group he attended. Tim happens to be a pastor, but he could have been anyone—a young mother looking for nonjudgmental support and empathy from a friend, a husband longing for a safe place to discuss what's really happening in his marriage, or an older woman wondering how to face life after the death of her husband. Tim's story echoes the experience of many looking for a safe place for genuine connection and unconditional love in the Christian community.

Tim's Story

"I feel so hurt and betrayed by the ministry right now, I'd like to resign," Tim said during a pastor's support group.

"What's going on?" someone asked.

"Well, for starters, I just lost several key leaders who have been loyal and heavily involved in our church—people I valued and trusted and depended on to stand with me."

"Join the club, bro, we've all been there," another said. "God is shaking the church and some people need to leave."

"Yeah," another man added. "Same thing happened to me last year. They come and they go. It's all part of the ministry. We just need to learn to guard our hearts and never fully trust anyone except the Lord."

The first man added, "I don't know if this fits for you or not, but I've learned never to 'lay hands on someone quickly' when it comes to leadership. I learned that from lots of hurt and disappointment in trusting the wrong people."

Tim listened patiently to the group's advice, feeling more and more frustrated and embarrassed by the moment. He had joined this group because he wanted a place where he could be transparent and vulnerable. He wanted a safe place where he could both give and receive encouragement, support, and mutual accountability. But this dialogue was not encouraging or supportive. In fact, he wished he could snatch back his words, along with his now-exposed vulnerabilities, and disappear through a crack in the floor.

Sound familiar? When a friend shares his or her pain or admits to a sin, are you quick to listen or are you quick to offer advice? Many believe they are expected to have the answers. David Seamands explains that in the first decade of his ministry he thought counseling was a "one-to-one preaching session with a captive audience."[3] His counsel consisted of telling the person what he *ought to be doing*—adding to the lie that everything depended on his ability to perform. He now realizes that the main task in helping someone is to help remove his or her barriers to experiencing God's grace. Removal of barriers to grace is often more a demonstration of God's unconditional love through listening than it is a declaration of the facts through speaking.

We all need a safe place to talk about our triumphs and tragedies, whether we've endured a terrible week of crises and stress, or whether we've been presented with a surprise bonus. We all can identify with the need to have a safe place to share; but unfortunately, we also can identify with suffering at the hands of "unsafe" people.

In contrast, here's a story that reminds us of the value of a listening friend. This account is again about Tim on what he called one of the worst days of his life. I, Dallas, happened to be the listener in this situation, but anyone using the listening skills in this book could have supplied the listening role.

Tim's Second Story

As I sat alone in my office, I suddenly felt a huge weight across my chest and I couldn't draw a deep breath. It felt like all the air was suddenly sucked out of the room. Could I reach the phone, I wondered. Should I dial 911?

Just then the phone rang and a familiar voice on the other end said, "How are things going? I haven't talked to you or seen you lately."

I managed to gasp out, "I think I'm coming apart."

"Well, brother, I'm here to listen," my friend, Dallas, said. "Tell me what's going on."

Although I could hardly speak at first, wondering if I needed an ambulance instead of a listener, I began to eke out some words. Dallas summarized what I said and invited me to "say more," occasionally asking me questions to keep me talking. I told him the story of the hell that had broken loose in my ministry in the past year—events that threatened to swallow me up in a black hole of humiliation and failure due to the betrayal of friends.

He kept me talking, and as I talked the panic subsided. I could take a deep breath once again. At the time I had no idea I was having a panic attack, or that I needed a listener—but when we were finished I felt great relief. More than that I was able to once again hear the quiet assurance of the Lord in my life and my ministry. My circumstances didn't change right away, but I was profoundly changed by that experience.

Tim was so impacted by this experience, and so disappointed by the lack of attention to listening in the pastor's support group he attended, he decided to find out what the Bible has to say about listening.

His search led him to the Book of Job, where three friends came to sympathize and comfort their friend. Unfortunately, these friends ended up "discomforting" Job instead. But good old Job was no pushover. He confronted his would-be helpers: "... miserable comforters are you all" (Job 16:2).

What did he mean by "miserable comforters"?

Job's wordy friends appear to have started out listening and ended up in what we call a "fixing frenzy." This frenetic activity is comparable to the "feeding frenzy" of circling, hungry sharks. A fixing frenzy occurs when a group begins to heap unsolicited advice on an already hurting person. "Will your long-winded speeches never end?" (16:3), Job asks of his circle of advisers. Clearly he was frustrated and wounded by their approach.

Certainly the compulsion to fix someone is not restricted to pastor's groups or to Job's companions. Human nature loves to offer the "winning" piece of advice—the wisdom that will bring a smile to the sad-faced friend, spouse, or child—as if you have entered some sort of "Best Advice of the Year " competition.

As Christians you and I can also justify our fixing frenzy with Scripture. We call it exhorting, teaching, admonishing, instructing, discerning—or the ultimate: "a word from the Lord."

However, we've observed that there is a high cost of *talking at* rather than *listening to* each other.

The Cost of Not Listening

When we do not listen, but jump into fixing, we say to the hurting person, "You may have struggled with this issue for hours (days, years), but I have the ability and wisdom to instantly solve your problem."

What's the cost? *The hurting person feels devalued and demeaned.* Perhaps that's what Solomon had in mind when he said, *"answering before listening is both stupid and rude"* (Prov.18:13, The Message).

Many Christians have years and years of experience and knowledge from Scripture and from life. They need help in finding the wisdom they *already possess*, not a lecture on what they already know.

When patient listening helps the hurting person find his or her God-given answers, negative feelings lift, faith "ears" open, and positive thoughts and feelings begin to surface.

Another cost of not listening is misunderstanding the person's situation altogether and *giving "stupid" advice*. Listening helps both the listener and the speaker get the whole picture. The hurting person often finds his own answer from the storehouse of his own resources in Christ; and with the telling of his story, the burden is lifted.

Still another cost of not listening is that you lose the opportunity to speak into the person's life when he really needs godly answers. Patient listening opens people's ears to what you have to say, while advice giving tends to "turn people off."

Your patient listening will create a bridge—an opportunity that will enable this person to receive your input when he really needs it. In a sense listening helps you earn the right to speak into someone else's life.

Giving the gift of listening doesn't mean going around selflessly and automatically being available to everyone you encounter. Rather it means being alert to those situations the Lord brings across your path when you are available and the person you're with needs to be heard.

Why Is It So Hard to Listen?

We have said that listening is hard because human nature loves to talk. Giving people our answers to their problems can make us feel powerful and important. In this section we will look more closely at why listening is so hard. We could sum it up in one word: *self*. Specifically self-reliance, self-centeredness, and self-condemnation.

Self-Reliance

Judy, a young brunette with three small children, had fallen on hard times. Her friend Stella told her, "How many times have you been there when I needed you? More than I can count. Now's my chance to help you, Judy."

Shaking her head, Judy said, "I really want to do this on my own, Stella. It's called self-reliance and that can't be wrong, can it?"

Is there anything wrong with self-reliance? From the beginning of history, human beings have proclaimed, "No!—self-reliance, can't be wrong!"

Adam said yes to self-reliance or independence when he made his own rules about eating the fruit from the tree of knowledge of good and evil. As a result of his choice, God put Adam and his family out of the garden. Ever since, mankind has followed Adam's example.

Casting off tyranny and establishing the Declaration of Independence was a good thing when our nation was born. Why? Because in God we trust was not an idle platitude but a strong governing value. History confirms that the Founding Fathers invited God to take over their hearts and minds as they established our nation. Since then, our nation has cast aside dependence on God—and in its place put the god of self-reliance. The cost in our relationship with God and other people has been enormous. "Cursed is the one who trusts in man, who depends on flesh for his strength and whose heart turns away from the Lord" (Jer. 17:5).

God responds favorably to people with childlike dependence. These individuals have ears tuned to His voice and hearts responsive to His love. They rest peacefully in full confidence that He will provide for their needs. God also values *interdependence* with others where each person acknowledges that he needs others as he depends on God. In fact He planned it so you and I couldn't succeed in the Christian life apart from interdependence with each other and total dependence on Him.

Upon Whom Do You Depend?

In our experience most people get this all mixed up. Some people are dependent on other people and not on God. Consider Susie, whose whole life revolved around her thirty-year-old son, Frank. She was so focused on his drug problem that she totally neglected her own spiritual, emotional, and physical needs. Time after time she came to his rescue, allowing him to drain her physically and financially.

At the opposite extreme, John believed that all he needed was his relationship with God. When his wife, Wendy, complained that he gave very little to her emotionally, he told her she needed to be spiritually strong and depend on God alone as he did. In reality John was so wounded as a child, he had vowed to never let anyone get close enough to hurt him again. His "Lone Ranger" attitude was a defense against risking an intimate, vulnerable relationship with another human being. He hid behind dependence on God alone in order to avoid intimacy with God's people.

Other people are not dependent on others—or on God; they are entirely dependent only upon themselves. They are often held up as the ideal in our culture. For example, take William, a cardiologist who built a large practice out of his own charm, skill, and determination. Highly respected in the church and in the community, he was a success in every way except in humble dependence on God and interdependence with the people of God.

Despite appearances to the contrary, in every life God works steadily and patiently to bring us to the end of our own ways. Only as we reach the end of our resources can we turn and rest in His ways. Only then can we give the gift of listening.

The Belief That Talking Is Power

Listening with patience and love is essential for both dependence on God and interdependence with others. Yet in our culture, talking is equated with mastery, power, and action—as in persuading, selling, teaching, evangelizing, preaching, counseling, or coaching. To listen to someone else means being out of the spotlight, out of the control position, and in the place of the learner—a position that is considered weak and undesirable.

Power Listening

After one of our seminars, Jason, a business owner and a father of three sons, exclaimed, "I'm amazed by what I've been learning from others. Since your seminar, I decided to listen to people without screening out or judging in advance who might have something worth hearing. I began to schedule listening times both at home and at work. I invited my sons to talk to me about what was going on in their lives. At work I invited people from every department to explain what would improve their work area. Through these listening times, I learned an astounding number of ways to increase the productivity of our company—but more importantly, to increase my effectiveness as a dad."

Value the Person Talking

If you don't value the person talking to you, then you are apt to tune him out. Barry is a young husband who works for a highly stimulating yet stressful advertising agency. He complained in a counseling session, "*My wife is boring. When I come home at night all Gloria talks about are the events in her day—like the kids, the toilet overflowing, and things like that. It feels bad to tune out her out, but the other people in my life are stimulating and interesting. I give her credit for trying to hear about my day, but she doesn't understand my world. I feel like we are growing further and further apart, and I don't know how much longer I can hang in there.*"

After listening in-depth to Barry's situation, we challenged him with the idea that Gloria could have some interesting things to say, provided he removed the mental barrier to hearing her. We asked Barry to learn how to listen to her through the filter of God's grace using listening skills. Later Barry told us that he began to reconsider her value as he listened and drew her into conversation. "*I discovered I really need what Gloria has to say. She has insights into people that I don't have—and as for her sensitivity to God … well, I'm weak there, too.*"

Charlie, a small group leader in a church care group, attended our seminar and told us about Sam and Betty who are in his group. "*In the beginning we wondered how they would work out because they weren't like the rest of us. They were kind of 'rude and crude,' if you know what I mean. Sam was loud and he talked a lot. He laid a lot of 'shoulds' and Bible verses on us even though his own marriage was a mess. I had to take him aside and gently confront him a couple times on how he came across to others.*

"But they kept coming back for more. And as we applied the gift of listening in the group, hearing one another's hearts and praying for each other, this couple began to soften and change. Recently Sam said to the group, 'I used to be arrogant, and I tried to impress people with how much I knew about the Bible. Now I'm learning to patiently listen and trust the Holy Spirit to do the convicting just like you all have done for me.' There were tears in the room as we listened to Sam's heart. God had placed them in our group not only so they could learn from us, but also so we could learn from them. We needed to learn that there is no 'them' and 'us.' We are all one in Christ Jesus. We all have value and we all have valuable things to share."

Understand the Power of Weakness

Many Christians believe the Bible says, "God helps those who help themselves." Yet this verse is not found in the Bible. Instead the opposite is true. "God helps the helpless."[4]

When the apostle Paul pleaded with God to have his weakness removed, the Lord responded, "… My grace is sufficient for you, for my power is made perfect in weakness" (2 Cor. 12:9).

Therefore, as you choose to trust the Lord to empower you to take the servant role as a listener, you land in a position of greater power. Instead of relying upon your own strength, you begin to operate in God's power through His grace—and in spite of your weakness.

Self-Centeredness

Another major listening barrier that is closely aligned with self-reliance is *self-centeredness*. Bill was a taker. Whenever you saw him with other people, he dominated the conversation. In any group setting, Bill craved attention and did whatever it took to place himself smack in the center of the limelight.

Bill came to us for counseling one day because he had no friends. "What's wrong with me?" he asked. As we attempted to understand how Bill interacted with others, we invited Kevin, his roommate, into a counseling session. Kevin said, *"When we get home after work, all Bill wants to talk about is his day. So in great detail he will tell me what was good and what was bad about it. At first, I tried to tell about some of the events in my day, but I quit trying to do that a long time ago. There is only one thing that interests Bill—and that's Bill."*

As Bill's history unfolded in our counseling session, we learned that when he was young no one listened to him or entered his world. His father was unavailable emotionally, and his mother worked long hours and was rarely around. Because of his childhood pattern, Bill learned to demand attention rather than wait for someone to give it to him.

The key challenge with self-centeredness is the lack of satisfaction. The self-centered person is never satisfied. Kevin, Bill's roommate, confided, *"At first I thought I could get a friendship going if I went the extra mile with him. And, I hate to say this, but the more I gave, the more he took. There's no end to it. Frankly, I'm looking for another roommate."*

One of the major results of self-centeredness is *loneliness*. People who are lonely often don't know how to put themselves aside for a long enough period to tune in to someone else's world. They have not learned that, in general, people are not interested in what you have to say until they are convinced that you understand and care about them and what they have to say.

Bill believed that love is lacking in the world and that you must demand what little you receive. His loneliness and selfishness were cured when he discovered that the source of endless love lives on the inside.

Self-centeredness is a primary relationship barrier between you and others, and between you and God. The attitude of self-centeredness robs you of the intimacy and impact God created for you to enjoy.

Self-Condemnation

Another barrier to listening is when people are tuned inward, listening to a flow of self-condemning thoughts. Their inner listening distracts them from absorbing the message when another person is talking. It's as if there's an invisible person next to them who is tearing them apart, dominating their attention so that the other's message can't get through. "Self-condemnation is that recurrent impression that you are not worth the love and care God desires to lavish on you."[5]

Harriet was bound in self-condemnation. *"No matter how loving others are to me, I can't fully receive it. No matter how deeply others accept me and genuinely appreciate me, I feel like I don't deserve it."*

As she began to "hear" what she said to herself, she recognized a voice contrary to what God, through the filter of his grace, says about her.

The voice of self-condemnation may sound familiar, like the voice of a father or mother. When someone learns to listen with more discernment, he recognizes Satan the Accuser energizing his self-rejection and destroying his ability to hear God and other people. (This topic is addressed in greater detail in chapter 10, Taking Thoughts Captive.)

Listening Styles That Create Barriers

Now we will turn to styles of listening that create barriers in relationships. There are three types of listening styles: *The Spock Listener, The Emotional Evader,* and *The Interrupter.* Each of these styles throws up barriers to listening.

The Spock Listener

Remember the pointed-ear Mr. Spock from "Star Trek" who was a logical walking computer? This alien character has many counterparts on planet Earth. These people are the intellectual listeners who listen with their heads, hear only what they want to hear, and then tune out large areas of reality. Walking through life, these people are unaware of their emotional impact on others. They also don't understand the impact of others on themselves. As they listen to their world, Spock listeners selectively make sure they hear only what doesn't disturb their internal system for maintaining order. Like data entering a computer, if something doesn't fit their logical sequence, their minds reject what is said as invalid. They are blind to their own emotions and the emotions of others.

Day in and day out, Hank worked as an engineer. His job demanded the analysis of information and he searched for design improvements. The way Hank handled his job carried over into all of his relationships. His wife, Michelle, described Hank as a nitpicker and someone who is overly critical. He constantly challenged her thought processes and tuned out her emotions. Hank's critical and unemotional listening approach brought him praise at work, yet the same approach made his family feel unappreciated and unloved. His ability to internally judge the comments of others didn't communicate the presence of a loving, accepting God who lived in and through him.

The Emotional Evader

At first glance, an emotional evader appears to have the emotional distance of the Spock listener. Yet upon closer examination, the emotional evader resists only certain topic—those that push his emotional "hot buttons." To reduce the feelings of frustration and confusion that these topics ignite, these people mentally flee from what is being said.

Pete and Rosemary have a blended family. One fall day, Pete suggested they take everyone to his family home in Michigan for Christmas. As the couple began to discuss the potential plans, Rosemary suddenly began talking about changing the floor in the kitchen and wondering when they would be able to redecorate. Pete wanted to continue with the holiday discussion but she insisted on talking about the pattern for the new kitchen floor. The discussion ended in an argument and nothing about vacation plans was determined. Later, Rosemary came into our counseling office and we revisited this argument. Rosemary is an emotional evader because she doesn't want to go to Michigan for Christmas and see her in-laws. She had never felt anything but resentment and hostility coming from them. Instead of confronting the hostility, Rosemary dealt with her situation through emotional evasion.

John was also an emotional evader. It didn't matter the topic but if the other person looked as if he was about to cry, John grew uncomfortable. When his wife cried, John never knew what to do. If he felt the conversation was getting into emotional territory, John tried to change the subject. If topic changing didn't work, he would suddenly disappear until "she got over it."

Many people with emotional pain have buried their own "hot spots" so they tune out others on a regular basis.

The Interrupter

When other people were talking, Phyllis habitually interrupted the conversation. Impulsively she interrupted for fear that she would forget what she wanted to say if she waited until the other person finished speaking. Because of her lack of consideration, other people felt devalued and reacted to Phyllis with frustration and annoyance.

During the listening seminar, Phyllis discovered that while others were talking, she was busy thinking about what she would say next. Because she didn't listen to the conversation, she tuned out the other person and didn't consider his needs. In a practice session of the seminar, Phyllis had to summarize what the other person said and she became aware of her pattern. As she anchored her life in the Lord and turned her fears over to God, Phyllis was able to concentrate intently and summarize what the other person said. She was also able to remember what she planned to say. As Phyllis learned to give the gift of listening, she discovered that her planned words were frequently unnecessary as she deeply listened to the other person's message.

Whether you or someone you know uses Spock Listening, Emotional Evasion, or Interruption, each type creates barriers to giving the gift of listening.

Messy Mixed Messages

Dale arranged to see his old college roommate, Jerry, at the Chicago airport because he had a long layover when changing planes. It had been years since the pair met, and they sat in a restaurant talking. While Dale launched into a long story about his family and children, Jerry seemed disinterested. Instead of focusing on Dale and looking at him, Jerry's eyes flitted back and forth at the people passing down the hallway. In the middle of his story, Dale said, "Well, you must not be very interested in what I have to say, Jerry."

Looking confused, Jerry sputtered, "What do you mean? I don't understand. I arranged to get off work early and made a special trip out here to see you. Why would you say I'm not interested?"

"Because you look a million miles away," Dale retorted. "Something in that hallway is much more important than what I have to say."

Jerry sent Dale a mixed message as he looked at his watch and the hallway rather than focusing on Dale and his story. You've heard the saying "actions speak louder than words?" Even though Jerry made an effort to see Dale and listen, his body language spoke louder than his words. Researchers are divided on how much of the message comes from words and how much from tone of voice, facial expression, posture, eye contact, and gestures.[6] One study said 7 percent for words, 38 percent for tone of voice, and 55 percent for the rest. Another said as much as 35 percent comes from words. Most agree that the impact of a person's nonverbal message is far greater than the words.

The skilled listener hears more than words. He listens to the voice tone and inflection. He notices expressions that convey tension, or distraction, or some other barrier—and he isn't afraid to check it out rather than jump to the wrong conclusion.

Each of these barriers exhibits our inadequacies when we are to listen to another person. We erect barriers not only because we don't know how to listen, but also because we are so focused on ourselves that we don't consider the impact on others.

In the next chapter we will consider a huge barrier to listening for many of us who have struggled in this area. We will look at our childhoods and how we were shaped as listeners.

Questions for Personal Reflection or Group Discussion:

- *How would you answer the question this chapter presents, "Why is listening so hard?"*

- *How do you relate to the story of Tim and the search for a safe place for genuine connection and unconditional love in the Christian community?*

- *Discuss your experience with any or all of the three styles of listening—Spock, Emotional Evader, or the Interrupter.*

- *How do "mixed messages" create barriers in relationships?*

4

The Shaping of a Listener

*More than we like to realize, we continue to live in the shadows
of the families we grew up in.*
Michael Nichols[7]

Your attitudes about listening began in the cradle. As you
lay in your crib and listened to the silence, it didn't fulfill your need
for Mom and Dad's attention. So you began to fuss and quickly
began to increase in volume until your entire little red body
hollered at the highest possible level. Clearly your "vocalizing"
skills were better developed than the baby equivalent of listening.

As you grew, the significant people in your life taught you more
about the value of listening. Here are some common messages you
may have heard.

"Stop crying or I'll give you something to cry about."
"Children should be seen and not heard."
"You shouldn't feel that way."

"You don't know what you're talking about."
"Shut up and listen."

Was your self-expression encouraged? Were you often told to "be quiet?" Did you often feel misunderstood and unappreciated?

The seeds of your current listening behavior were sown in childhood. If your parents listened to your needs, appreciated them, then responded to your communication attempts, you probably grew up feeling worthwhile. "Being listened to helps build a strong, secure self."[8] If the opposite was true, you may feel insecure about who you are and your ability to influence your world.

Examples of how parents build or destroy self-assurance are everywhere. In the park is the mother who kneels down to her child with love in her eyes, then listens to a secret or extends comfort over a bruised knee. Or in the supermarket, we see the father who reduces his child to tears of rage for making a mistake. As these experiences occur over and over, they shape the child—as well as the adult he or she will become. As you look at how you were shaped as a listener, our prayer for you is that you will not only rejoice in how God has changed you, but also that you will surrender quickly those negative self-talk patterns that still entangle and trip you up today. God is in the business of molding His children. You will find, as you consider how you were shaped as a listener, that there is nothing He will not change if you invite Him to do so.

Sometimes parents are too preoccupied, depressed, or distracted to attend to the "messages" from their little one. When Mom and Dad have prolonged periods of ignoring a bright-eyed baby, they begin the long, sad process of wilting the child's sense of value as well as the child's ability to connect with others. Infant researcher Daniel Stern found that our need for understanding is our second greatest need, and only the need for food and shelter is higher.[9] Even babies need listening to flourish.

Michael Nichols in *The Lost Art of Listening* gives the example of an inquisitive baby perched on a parent's lap and the child attempts to explore the mysteries of the parent's mouth or nose.

Then the child pulls on the parent's hair to see if it will detach. If the parent interprets this behavior as aggressive or annoying, he might scold or slap the baby. If the child's repeated attempts to explore are met with parental hostility, the baby begins to believe that exploration is bad. "Misunderstanding undermines not only our trust in others, but also our trust in our own perceptions."[10]

Parents' listening behaviors are modeled for the children. Children mimic the behavior of adults. Parents can communicate disrespect, judgment, or withdrawal through posture, or facial expressions like the rolling of the eyes, or verbal free-for-alls where everyone talks and no one listens. Or perhaps they isolated from one another and focused their attention on the child. Or they ignored the child as well as each other. Whatever the communication patterns, people tend to duplicate throughout their lives the patterns they learned in their early years.

Darcy couldn't understand her reluctance to grow emotionally close with her husband, Jim. "When my husband begins to talk about his feelings, why do I get uncomfortable?" she asked during a counseling session. "It's almost like I pick a fight to distract him so I'm not forced to listen to his feelings. I saw my mother do the same thing with my dad."

"When Jim begins to share about himself, what emotion do you feel?" I asked.

"Fear," Darcy said without hesitation.

Darcy grew up with a father who had a violent temper. When he expressed feelings, family members got hurt. This behavior pattern created a strong belief that still gripped her adult behavior: listening to emotions results in pain.

Dallas and Nancy's Childhoods

As we (Dallas and Nancy) reflected on our own childhoods, each of us had different listening experiences as a child.

I (Nancy) remembered my preoccupied mother who often didn't see or hear me. She was locked in an unhappy marriage with my

father. Consequently both my parents were more focused on bat-
tling each other than they were on listening to my brother and me.
Once when I was small, I wanted Mother's attention but she sat
and stared into space. *She was not busy,* I reasoned. *Why wouldn't
she hear me?* "Mom?" I said. She didn't respond. So I spoke a little
louder, " Mom?" Without blinking an eye, Mother continued to
stare into space. I began to panic and escalated the volume of my
speaking until I was nose-to-nose in her face screaming,
"Motherrrrrrr!"

Suddenly she jerked into the present as if I had struck a raw
nerve and yelled as she shook me, "What's *wrong* with you? Don't
you ever do that again!"

This "tuning out" behavior left me believing that my thoughts
and feelings were unimportant and that I had nothing of significance to contribute to the lives of others.

In stark contrast, I (Dallas) had a listening mother along with
my grandmother who lived with us. Either woman would often lay
down her work so she could tune into me with love and acceptance
shining from her eyes. Consequently, I grew up with the belief that
I had something of value to contribute to those around me. Because
of this early influence, it's not surprising that years later, a Christian
doctor brought me into his OB/GYN practice. My marriage and
family counselor offices shared the suite with his practice. If he
believed his patients needed a listening ear and some emotional
help, which was common with OB/GYN patients, then he walked
them down the hall and into my office. I built a practice of listening to women pour out their hearts.

Parents as Listeners

The way in which adults listen to children teaches children
something about themselves. "Parents who interrupt their children,
look stern while listening, ignore their children's feelings, or turn
away when the children are talking send a message that what the
children have to say is stupid or unimportant."[11] This negatively

impacts the child's self-image—an impact that continues into adulthood. As a result, listening ability is impaired. "Studies show that when people are anxious or worried about approval, they have trouble concentrating on what is being said."[12]

Bill had trouble concentrating when people in authority spoke to him. Consequently he often missed instructions and sometimes made costly mistakes. During our seminar he realized the source of this troubling behavior. When he was a child, his father often frowned when Bill talked. Without his father saying a word, Bill believed he did not measure up to his dad's expectations. The same anxiety he felt as a child still interfered with his ability to listen as an adult.

Three Roles People Hide Behind

When people grow up without loving, understanding listeners who can mirror the child's value and worth, they may take on rigid roles to hide their own sense of inadequacy and to protect themselves.

Eric Berne talks about three such patterns of behavior: *persecutor*, *rescuer*, and *victim*.[13]

The Persecutor

Persecutors determine to control others rather than to be controlled. They manipulate those people around them through fault finding and nit-picking. Rather than listening to understand your viewpoint, they are thinking about how to refute what you say. They are negative thinkers who zero in on how something is going to fail or cannot possibly work. When communicating with a persecutor, often you feel as though you are treated like a stupid child.

In one of our listening seminars, a participant talked about a former boss. "This guy was never happy with any of our work. He seemed to thrive on telling us what we did wrong, then ignoring anything good about our efforts. When we made mistakes, from his reaction, you'd think we deserved the electric chair. Am I glad I don't work for him any-

more! Ironically not a single one of my coworkers continued working there either."

The Rescuer

On the other hand, rescuers want to help other people, often by giving advice. They will rescue an individual whether or not the person asks for assistance. Like persecutors, these individuals operate from low self-worth. Rescuers attempt to find significance through helping others.

Because their self-worth depends on being needed, they foster dependent relationships. When someone depends on a rescuer, it inhibits his ability to learn and solve his own problems, think on his own, and make independent decisions.

As you are talking to a rescuer, the rescuer is thinking about how to solve your problem instead of listening to you. Because he is not concentrating on your message, he doesn't get an accurate picture of your situation. As a result, often he gives unwise or inappropriate advice. Rescuers may serve others through the role of friend, pastor, counselor, or other service, yet their assistance to others springs from their own self-centered need to feel needed.

While attending a listening seminar, Darin, a pastor, realized that he often listened and behaved as a rescuer. He confessed, "My motive was to interrupt and to give you some kind of Band-Aid for your problem. In advance, I could tell you everything you were going to say, so you would understand that I read you properly. Then I'd whip some answers on you and send you out the door. I called it the gift of discernment."

As one of eight children from an alcoholic father, Darin began to understand a large part of his motive in ministry was to fill the hole in his heart left by his father's rejection. Today Darin has turned over the rescuing role to the Wonderful Counselor. As a result the Holy Spirit accomplishes astonishing healing and restoration through Darin's ministry.

Rescuers can easily find themselves overworked and unappreciated. The person they are helping may turn on them because they didn't give the "right" advice, or because they weren't available at all hours to meet endless needs. Until they find God's healing from this bondage, rescuers often discover they are buried in the problems of people and falling victim to the same group of people they are trying to assist.

The Victim

Victims expect to be mistreated. These individuals seem to invite this mistreatment from others almost as if they are wearing a "Kick Me" sign. They welcome persecution and allow their self-worth to be tied to responses from other people. Instead of anchoring their lives in Christ, victims are adrift, blown about from the inconsistency and immaturity of other people. They find themselves being pulled out of the rescuer role, changing into the victim role, then finally moving into the persecutor role. They become tormented with bitterness toward the people God has called them to love.

Here's an example of a rescuer pastor who first fell into the victim role, then became the persecutor:

One day, Pastor James called me (Dallas) regarding an experience with a former church member, Harry.

Pastor James explained that a few years back, he had spent an extraordinary amount of time helping Harry, whose life was falling apart. To the pastor's amazement, Harry then suddenly dropped out of the church. Just recently, Pastor James had received a phone call and then a visit from Harry. Harry began the session by saying, "I'm troubled because of something that happened between us and I want to clear it up." Interested in resolving this situation and helping Harry, Pastor James listened. During this conversation, it became clear that Harry had assumed that Pastor James would continue the intense interaction at a time when Harry was in the hospital, and he had been waiting for a phone call from the pastor. When Pastor James didn't call, Harry felt deeply hurt and began to attend another church.

Pastor James tried to give Harry a dose of reality. His church has 250 people and probably 50 of them needed his attention at any one time. The pastor told Harry, "If I spent the same amount of time with each of them as I had with you, it would take two years to get through my list."

Harry said, "You deceived me, Pastor. I shared things with you in a more honest manner than I have ever done with anyone else. As we met together, somehow I found the courage to face my problems knowing that you would be there to support me in the future. Now I feel deceived from your lack of attention. In fact, I wonder how many other people you have deceived with your listening ear through the years!"

The vicious words from Harry left Pastor James dumbstruck with this man's insensitivity and ingratitude. As the final straw, Harry sent a letter of complaint to Pastor James' church board.

As we continued to talk, Pastor James said, "... I'm concerned some of the board members will think there's some validity to Harry's complaints." Then he hung his head and shook it saying, "What do the people want from me? I give and give and yet it never is enough." In the process of this experience, Pastor James had moved from the role of rescuer to persecutor to victim.

Sometimes you can play the victim role in certain areas of your life, yet not in others. Let's consider the story of Wilma—who understood she was acting like a victim in relation to her computer skills for her new business.

Wilma was working with Jack to gain some technical expertise with the computer. Patiently Jack would explain how to create computer files, then watch her do it and leave the room. Within ten minutes, Wilma had forgotten Jack's explanations. In her mind, Wilma had no idea how to proceed on the computer, so she called Jack and asked him to explain it again.

Again Jack explained the different functions and Wilma thought she understood. Yet when he walked away, she again drew a blank and called a third time for his help. Repeatedly Jack taught Wilma every new computer skill.

One day Jack changed from his patient response and confronted Wilma, "I'm not helping you anymore because you never really listen to *me. No matter how many times I show you these computer functions, it doesn't stick. How a reasonably intelligent woman can be so dense is beyond me. What's your problem?"*

Later, through the listening seminar, Wilma realized why she struggled and was scared to learn computers or any other technical matter. Any time Jack gave her instructions, Wilma was thinking to herself, *I'll never understand what he's telling me. I must be incredibly stupid in this area.* She felt despair, but through the listening seminar she understood the root cause. As Jack was teaching her, Wilma wasn't listening to him but only hearing the negative tapes playing inside her head. In her family, Wilma grew up as the baby in the family. From an early age, she learned that no one listened to her or took her actions with any seriousness. Her role in the family was to act cute, helpless, dumb, and dependent on others.

A multitude of factors have shaped your life, including your childhood experiences, beliefs, expectations, attitudes, assumptions, values, and prejudices. Each of these aspects serves as a filter for your life experiences. These filters help form your self-image, which is the filter through which you determine your identity and what is possible for your actions. These filters influence our listening skills as adults. For each person, it is valuable to examine your beliefs, values, attitudes, and expectations.

Where do you find the strength necessary to break down these barriers?

Breaking Down Barriers

In our search for strength to listen, let's consider how Jesus dealt with His disciples in the Upper Room. As David and Teresa Ferguson point out, Jesus gathered the Twelve around the Passover meal only a few hours before His arrest, and something unusual happened. Jesus removed His outer garment, wrapped a towel around His waist, poured water in a basin, and washed His disciples' feet. "He was only hours away from an agonizing death, and yet he spent precious minutes washing their dirty feet. Do the disciples deserve this loving touch?"[14]

Even as He served them, the disciples began to exhibit blatant self-centeredness, self-reliance, and self-condemnation. James and John tried to assert their importance with an argument over who was the greatest, yet Jesus tenderly washes their feet. He didn't scold them or lecture them on their need to follow His example.

Peter asserted his self-reliance, when he says, "No, Lord," when Jesus approached his feet. "You don't need to wash my feet."

Jesus responded, "If I do not wash you, you have no part with me" (John 13:8).

Another disciple, Judas, had already betrayed his Lord for thirty pieces of silver. He sat at the table under a cloud of self-condemnation. His guilt soon drove him to take his own life. But Jesus also washed his feet with the same tenderness He had for the others.

Jesus does much more than wash our feet. He has cleansed us through and through with His own righteousness. God's Spirit leads us to the heart of Jesus as He encounters our sinful patterns. He doesn't leave us or throw up His hands in disgust. He touches us tenderly, washes us, changes us, and ministers love to us.

I know all about your needs, Jesus lovingly says. *I understand your helplessness to remove self-focus from your relationships. I love you, and your concerns are my concerns. I will always be present to meet your needs right on time. You don't have to take; just receive. Will you, by faith, trust in My love, relax your grip on what you want, and allow Me to change you and to meet your needs according to My will and My schedule?*

Just knowing what Jesus would do is not enough. Whether you struggle with self-condemnation, self-reliance, or self-centeredness, the same Jesus who humbly washed His disciples' feet now lives on the inside of you if you have received Him. He is the only one who can live the Christian life. Are you ready to let Him take down the barriers and do the listening and the living through you?

5

Discovery Listening Skills

We have this hope as an anchor for the soul, firm and secure ...
Hebrews 6:19a

Here's a handy way to conceptualize discovery listening skills. Each finger represents an element of discovery listening. *(See figure 1, p. 60)*

Anchoring

The thumb reminds us that anchoring is the starting point for listening. Because the thumb is an essential portion of the hand for grasping any object, anchoring on the indwelling presence of Christ is critical to the listening process.

Focusing

The second finger on the hand reminds you to focus. When you use a camera to focus a picture, you adjust the lens until the focal

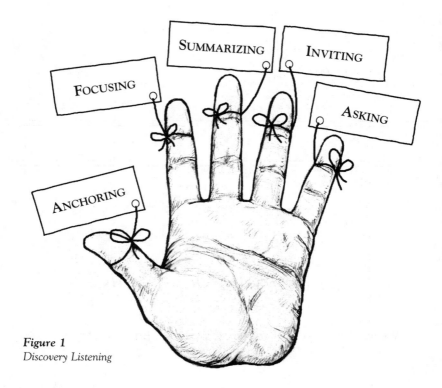

Figure 1
Discovery Listening

point of the picture stands in sharp contrast to the background and the fuzzy edges disappear.

Summarizing

The middle finger represents summarizing, which is central to the listening process. Summarizing is simply rephrasing what you hear into your own words without changing the meaning.

Inviting

The ring finger represents the skill of inviting. After you have summarized for the speaker and he seems to be finished, invite him to "say more." This skill moves the speaker deeper into self-discovery. If you begin to give your own message before you invite and ask, the speaker may not say something that really needs to be said.

Asking

The final finger on the discovery listening hand is a powerful means to continue to explore additional heart territory with the speaker. Through the inviting technique, you can take the conversation deeper, but through asking open questions you can help the speaker make full disclosure for his own discovery and relief.

Each of these skills will be described in more detail in this chapter and the chapters that follow.

The Anchored Listener

If you didn't have a thumb, consider the challenge to pick up a baseball bat, grip it firmly, and hit the ball out of the park. As a thumb secures your grip, anchoring secures the listening process. It is essential to listening and to your ability to live the Christian life.

"Do you know, my friends, that the spirit within you is very God? ... I could shout for joy as I think, 'The Spirit who dwells within is no mere influence, but a living Person; he is very God. The infinite God is within my heart!'"[15]

We have said that the gift of listening moves us beyond the place where in our own strength we say, "I can do this." Our past conditioning and our preoccupation with self continually defeat us, even though we want to change and may have tried many times to shape up as communicators. In other words, ultimately listening is an act of God. It requires that you and I abandon our own strength and "try harder" mentality and rest in the indwelling Christ. Jesus was the greatest listener imaginable and He is the One who listens to us when we feel we have nothing worth hearing. It is only as we discover how to appropriate the communicating power of Jesus that we become gifted listeners. He gives us a hearing heart and an understanding mind.

The Importance of an Anchor

When you throw an anchor overboard, it goes straight to the bottom and secures the ship to the ocean floor. Surface wind and waves may threaten to carry the ship away. Currents may tug and pull the vessel this way and that, but a strong anchor secures the ship and ensures the safety of everyone on board.

Likewise, the storms of life tear at Christian relationships and desire to destroy the home, the church, and drown the occupants. But anchoring in Christ secures individuals who are rooted and grounded in the safety of God's love and assurance of His presence. On our own power or steam we cannot live the Christian life, let alone listen to an angry partner, a disgruntled church member, a hysterical child, an irritating neighbor, or a pompous and disrespectful boss. Apart from Christ living through you and me, we can't accomplish these actions.

Anchoring involves resting in the presence of Jesus, the Wonderful Counselor, inside of you whether you are speaking or listening. As you listen while someone drains off his "stuff," life-transforming discoveries can occur in one or both of you. This happens in any situation in which one or more participants rest or anchor the communication in the hands of the Wonderful Counselor.

The concept of anchoring is graphically shown through a story that Steve Farrar tells about a couple.[16] One sunny day this pair sailed the Pacific in their twenty-foot sailboat. They were aware of a hurricane several hundred miles away but believed it was headed in another direction so they thought they were perfectly safe. But hurricanes are unpredictable and it turned about-face and headed straight for them. Despite the increasing winds, the couple still believed they would be okay. So they dropped their two anchors in a bay close to one of the Marshall Islands and determined to ride out the storm, playing cards, and drinking coffee.

When the winds and gigantic waves hit full force first one anchor chain snapped, then the other and they were swept away. Systematically, the storm ripped their ship apart and eventually the woman lost her life. If this couple had been waiting out the storm on the USS *Dwight D. Eisenhower*, one of the largest ships in the world, they would have not been in danger. This huge aircraft carrier, which is the size of a twenty-two-story building, contains two anchors weighing 60,000 pounds each. One link in the huge anchor chain weighs 365 pounds. As an anchor is a critical part of every ship, it's critical for every person to be anchored in his or her relationship with Jesus Christ.

After over thirty years of counseling, we have learned an extremely important lesson. Unless God shows up in the counseling room, not much will change in the long-term view of a person's life. However, we have grown increasingly aware of God's continual presence. The Holy Spirit lives in the hearts of those who have trusted Christ as Savior. Out of the provision of His grace, the Lord not only saved us but He has made His home within us. We appropriate the power and energy of His presence and trust Him to continually fill and surround us with His presence. Anchoring is our acknowledgment of this unseen reality. It is trusting Christ to animate and energize the communication process.

God's presence for both the listener and the speaker means that each one can be changed. The person who listens is also learning. Through listening, this person is not only learning about the speaker's story, but often the listener discovers his own story and what God is saying to him as he listens to the speaker.

As you anchor your life in Christ, this choice isn't only about listening but turning your living over to His powerful indwelling presence. "In Christ" you are anchored, secured, and animated by His enabling presence. And because you are anchored, you are enabled to listen and speak with confidence, skill, and respect.

By Faith, Draw on the Patience and Love of the Indwelling Christ

Once the truth of "Christ in you" gets hold of you, no one and nothing can destroy your composure, even under fire. In other words, in Christ, when you feel attacked or somehow demeaned by another person, you can choose not to react because of your security in the One who is your life. When Jesus was on earth, He lived each day in the security of His Heavenly Father. In the same way, because He lives in you and longs to live through you, you can rest each day—and each exchange—in His hands. Your worth is not at stake. Your peace and confidence need not be shaken because of anything you hear. Anchoring expresses the humble, gentle, patient, kind, bold, confident, vulnerable, transparent, forgiving, respectful, courageous Christ in you.

We're not saying you will achieve sinless perfection. On occasion, you will lose your cool. Yet even when you lose it, you will know how to quickly return to the rest, security, and power because of your awesome identity in the One who is the source of your Christian life.

As you are anchored in Christ, you can live with confidence— "not because of your *profession* of Christ as Savior but because of your *possession* of Christ as life" says Steve McVey. Anchoring allows the indwelling, enabling presence of Christ to animate and energize your life. As you understand this bond or anchor with Christ, you enter a place of *trusting* Him to live through you rather than *trying* to live for Him.

The apostle Paul said, "In Christ, you are complete" (Col. 2:9,10). He actually said, "You have been given fullness," and the word fullness means complete, secure, "anchored." The thesaurus enriches and expands the meaning of the word "fullness" with the following synonyms: glutted, gorged, sated, brimming, crammed, stuffed, chock-full, bursting, stocked, crowded, teeming, saturated, overflowing.

When you are complete, there is no desperate need for anyone to give you something to make you whole—love, appreciation, or security—because you already have it all *in Christ*.

Are you tired of the struggle? Are you ready to say and to mean: *"I'm giving up. I can't—I won't—go on. Surely there is more to life than what I am experiencing."*

Are You Desperate Enough to Allow Christ to Take Over?

Possibly at this point, you are saying, "God, you designed the Christian life so it must be a good thing, but my relationships are so empty and so painful. Please, God, take this mess and make it the way you intended life to be."

Have you come to the end of your own resources? Then rejoice because you have arrived at a good place in life. Our observation in our own life and the lives of those whom we serve is that most Christians eventually come to the *end of their own resources*—their ability to meet the circumstances in their lives—before they are willing to let God take over.

"God frequently has to knock the bottom out of our experience to get us in direct contact with Himself." Oswald Chambers.[17]

How about you? What is your frustration level? Are you tired of trying? Maybe you work hard to keep the illusion of the ideal Christian, for the sake of your ministry or your reputation in the church. But day-by-day you are growing increasingly more frustrated because of the gap between what you believe your life could be and what is happening in your life.

Are You Ready to Give Up?

Jesus said, "Apart from me you can do nothing" (John 15:5).

Webster's dictionary says *nothing* means: that which does not exist; a nonentity; absence of all magnitude or quantity; a zero.[18] Some people take a long time to finally agree that they can do nothing. Some people want to argue with God. They say, "But, Lord, aren't there some things I can do on my own?"

When Jesus Christ walked the earth, the Savior could do nothing apart from God. How much help do *you* need to get your life straightened out? For that matter, how much do you need God to do anything? Are you ready to admit you need someone to help you and you need someone to do it all for you? Are you ready for someone to take over your relationships, your communication, your life?

As you appropriate God's gift of grace, His life animating your life, it begins with this decision. Then you live out this decision in daily communication challenges in which you will return to this decision to rest your life in His indwelling presence.

Here's how Claire responded to the challenge. Claire and Tom owned and operated a small business. The pressures of getting the business off the ground plus being business owners/partners for twenty-four hours a day with little outside help had taken an emotional toll on their marriage. Often when either one got discouraged the other person forgot to listen and tried a "quick fix" through advice giving or some form of motivation so the person would climb out of his depression. Using these ineffective techniques usually led the couple into resentment and a verbal battle. Or they got into a "can you top this" mode and each one unloaded his pain at the same time so no one listened. As a result, Claire and Tom often became even more discouraged and alone after their "discussions." Each of them had self-medicated their pain through overeating, which only added self-disgust to their pile of discouragement.

One day Claire decided to turn the conversation over to the Lord and give Tom the gift of listening. Tom walked into the room and said, "I constantly feel like a failure. When our business thrives, I feel guilty about not having time to plan for the future. When business slows, I am too worried to plan for the future. Also I feel like a failure as a dad, plus I've failed to lose my weight, and I have an inability to be a kind and understanding person with you, Claire, as we work together. I hate going to work, and I just want to escape when I'm home. I feel like I'm falling apart."

As Tom began to talk, Claire thought, *This is too heavy for me. He really is falling apart and I don't want to hear it because I'm scared about our business, too. He needs to talk to a counselor.* But then I thought, *Nonsense. I have the Wonderful Counselor living in me. I will choose to anchor in Christ and just listen to Tom.* So she did. She focused, summarized, invited (using the skills you will learn in the next two chapters), and reminded herself throughout that her part was to "rest" and let Christ work through Tom's conversation. As she gave the gift of listening, Claire felt a peace settle over her even though Tom was getting deeper and deeper into his pain. His words were hard to hear because they triggered so many of her issues.

More than once she wanted to interrupt him and tell him that she felt the same way. Throughout the conversation, she continued to thank the Lord for animating the exchange as she used the listening skills. When he was finished, she asked if she could interject a question. Upon affirmation she asked him, "If someone came to you with these issues, what would you say to him?"

For a long moment, he thought about the question and then said, "I guess I'd say you need to keep your eyes on the Lord. You need to give grace to yourself. You need to stop listening to the enemy's lies and start telling yourself the truth about who you are in Christ." She continued to use the listening skills until he had compiled a hefty list of godly wisdom from his own counsel from the mind of Christ.

When he was completely finished, he looked so relaxed and satisfied that she wondered if he might fall asleep. She asked if he'd be willing to listen to her perspective for another twenty minutes.

He said he would gladly listen to her. Claire shared her similar feelings of failure in her impatience at times with him. She also told about her resentment toward their business, her weight, and her concern that she also was not a good enough parent. With each revelation, he focused, paraphrased, and invited her to say more. When she finished, he asked her the same question that he had faced, "What would you tell someone else who came to you with these issues?"

Then she shared her belief that God was turning the heat up in their business and marriage so they would have to turn to the Lord as their only source. Tom held to the gift of listening and didn't revert to his old pattern. In the past Tom would argue or get defensive or accuse Claire of telling him how to think or feel. This time he listened to her and asked, "Is there anything else?"

Afterward they prayed and reflected on how freeing it felt to know each one was tempted with the same crummy thoughts and runaway emotions. The couple marveled at how they each could hear the voice of God when they filtered out the interfering garbage and didn't blame each other. More than any time in recent memory, Claire and Tom felt close to each other because they anchored themselves in God's grace and gave each other the gift of listening.

As Claire reflected on the incident, she was struck with the power of her own choice in this matter. If she had not chosen from the beginning to trust Christ, the conversation could have easily ended in a verbal battle and cold withdrawal as in the past. As she let Christ take over, it changed the whole tone of their evening. They felt more prepared to return to work the next morning with renewed love for each other and energy for their business.

Claire's story illustrates several important truths about the gift of listening:

It allows God's grace to transform your need to control and fix others.

It offers an alternative to withdrawing into self-gratification and self-medicating as a means of solving your relationship pain.

It shows the power of one person choosing to believe that not only is Christ her life, but He is also her husband's life. And that when she listened while anchored in Christ, the wisdom and love in her husband could surface to supply what he needed. She was not responsible for "fixing" him.

You can be a safe person for your partner, your friends, your children, and your coworkers. You might even be a person who is a magnet for other people in your church because you have the reputation of being a good listener. You'll find yourself listening to the heart of unbelievers and earning the right to share your life in Christ with them. Through listening, you can also invite others to listen to you so that you have a safe place to discover and receive God's healing touch, too. We need each other.

Through listening, you can:

- *Reduce stress*
- *Show love*
- *Minimize misunderstanding*
- *Relieve anger, fear, loneliness, and pain*
- *Clarify direction*

- *Stop a power struggle*
- *Create a bond*
- *Lead someone to Christ*
- *Repair a marriage*
- *Make a friend*
- *Express the grace of God*
- *Receive the grace of God as another listens to you*

Listening will provide many benefits to your life.

Some Additional Thoughts to Consider

The Bible addresses life from two vantage points. First, there is the law or behavioral rules, which we could call the *head change*. Second, we have grace, the Spirit of Christ, living on the inside and accomplishing the *heart change*.

It is not enough to have one part without the other. If we know the rules or guidelines for the Christian life, it does not mean that you and I can live it. In fact, the Bible clearly states the laws (behavioral rules) do not produce the righteousness of God (Gal. 2:15,16). In the same way, knowing the rules of how to communicate does not produce loving, unselfish, patient communicators.

Trying to live up to the laws of God brings us to an end of our own attempts to measure up. Bible scholars call this legalism or attempting to meet God's requirements through our own performance. Psychology calls it being performance driven. Whatever you call it, the experience will tie you hopelessly into knots with no way out unless you allow the only One who *can* live the Christian life to live through you.

"Those who trust God's action in them find that God's Spirit is in them—living and breathing God! Obsession with self in these matters is a dead end; attention to God leads us out into the open, into a spacious, free life" (Rom. 8, *The Message*).

Although we're going to increase your capacity to listen as we teach you the communication skills beginning in the next chapter, please remember that applying the skills alone can result in a cold and unfriendly exercise. These skills can become like the Old Testament Law or a list of powerless rules apart from the presence of God to animate them and you. In fact, these skills can be used to manipulate, control, or wound another person as cruelly as you ever did before you knew how to use them. Without grace, this skill set can become weapons, or at the very least, powerless to impact your relationships—except in the negative sense.

In summary, the first discovery listening skill, *anchoring*, is the power source for giving the gift of listening. It is a decision that you will return to again and again as you choose to trust each exchange to the One who is your life.

In the following chapter you will learn about the next two fingers on the hand diagram—*focusing* and *summarizing*.

Questions for Personal Reflection or Group Discussion

• *How would you define the term "anchoring"?*

• *How do you relate to the story of Tom and Claire?*

• *How could the process of anchoring yourself in Christ impact your relationships? What role has hardship played in your learning to anchor in Christ? Where are you in the process of relying on Christ to live through you?*

6

Are You Ready to Listen?

Fundamentals of Listening

Eric closed his newspaper and said with an edge to his voice, "Okay, I'll listen. What do you want to say?" All day Carol had been waiting to talk to him about the fears and frustrations from her first day at work, but something stopped her. Eric had promised he would listen, but he rolled his eyes as he put the paper down.

"What's wrong with you?" Carol asked.

Eric sounded on the defensive, "What do you mean what's wrong with me? I'm listening. Let's have it. What do you want to say?"

"I can't talk to you," she replied and stomped out of the room in anger.

With a confused look on his face, Eric walked after her. "Hey, I was willing to listen. What's your problem?"

His lips said one thing, but his nonverbal communication gave a different message: "Don't bother me."

We are complex beings, capable of sending complex and often confusing messages. And the knots of our relationships are directly influenced by the tangles on the inside or the inner conflict within our heart, mind, will, and emotions.

When you are in the midst of conflict, your body has a way of "telling on you." It leaks information that you may not want it to say. Sometimes you are not even aware that the conflict is evident to anyone else. For example, Eric was unaware that his body was talking and that his nonverbal expressions conflicted with his words. His body language seemed to say, "Leave me alone," though his actual words were "I'm listening."

Carol responded in a natural manner. When someone is deciding which message is the truth—the actual words or what you see and tone of voice—research shows most people respond to the nonverbal message. Carol walked away feeling hurt and anger from the tone of Eric's voice and the way he rolled his eyes.

"The reason we don't recognize the impact of our tone of voice is that we hear what we feel like, not what we sound like."[19]

In this chapter and the next, you will continue to learn how to avoid the painful disconnects Eric and Carol experienced, as you understand how to apply discovery listening skills.

Let's return to our handy diagram of discovery listening skills.[20]

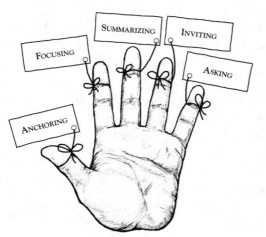

The Focused Listener

When you listen, you want the person talking to be front and center in your line of vision. You want the other person to know that you are intently listening and fully engaged in the conversation.

In the opening story, Eric used words to say he was ready to talk, but his body language did not agree with his words. The first step in the skill of focusing involves determining *"Am I able to focus right now?"* and *"Do I want to listen right now?"* If you don't want to listen for any reason, it's better to communicate this reluctance rather than send a mixed message, which leaves both participants feeling hurt and confused.

Eric could have said something like, "My head's not into hearing you right now, Carol. Nothing personal. I'm just bummed out at the moment. Give me twenty minutes to regroup and I'm all yours." If Eric had used this type of message, Carol wouldn't have to wonder which message to choose: what he said or what he did. And she could choose to respond differently. Possibly Carol could have offered to listen to Eric for a short time and help him deal with his bummed-out feelings. And if later in the day Eric doesn't offer to talk, Carol can ask for a specific time when his head and his heart are ready to listen.

Are You Ready to Listen?

Because listening requires your full attention and adequate energy, tell the speaker if you are too tired to do justice to what he wants to say to you. Listening is hard work and requires heavy concentration along with committed energy. One element that causes fatigue for the listener is that you can process information at around three hundred to five hundred words per minute. Speakers, however, can only talk at about two hundred words per minute.[21] Therefore your mind tends to wander—daydreaming, going on mental tangents, or working on other pressing issues in your life.

If you are too tired or distracted at the moment the speaker wants to talk, then say so. No one, except God, can always be on call for listening. The important thing is that you know how to listen and are committed to using your skills in the relationship. Tell the speaker that you want to hear him, but at a later time. Then schedule a specific time when you will be available. If you are rarely—or never—available to listen to the other person, perhaps the relationship is not a high priority in your life.

How Long to Listen

When you are ready to listen, establish the length of time you will commit to listening. The reason we suggest a time limit is because listening is hard work. It is active rather than passive in nature, requiring intense concentration and focus. People often think they should be able to "talk until the matter is settled." This assumption sets them up for failure. As energy drains and emotions escalate, they often fall back into the old, destructive habits that got them into trouble in the first place.

Although we (Dallas and Nancy) spend many hours listening to people, when it comes to our own relationship, we can only handle about twenty to thirty minutes of intense concentration at optimum energy. After that, we need a break to recharge. Since many issues need more than twenty or thirty minutes to work through, we reschedule a time to resume. As we coach others who are working through relationship issues, they also benefit from the twenty- to thirty-minute guideline. If you need more time, it's better to reschedule for a later time than to continue past your prime. Short, intense, focused times of listening can accomplish more than years of casual listening when it comes to resolving issues and strengthening your relationships.

There are some additional factors that help you get ready to listen.

Set the Scene

You can turn off the television, empty your hands, turn off the phones, or close your office door if you are at work. In other words, you can consciously deal with any distractions in your environment. These concrete actions send a powerful I-care-about-you message to the other person. If you have children in the setting, try to occupy them elsewhere so you'll have uninterrupted time. Now that you are ready to listen, pay attention to your body language. What are you saying nonverbally that might distract the speaker?

Open Posture and Eye Contact

Turn and face the speaker with arms and legs uncrossed. This stance sends the nonverbal message that your head and your heart are in agreement with your decision to listen. Look at the speaker. This states nonverbally that you are attentive and actively involved. Looking at the speaker also ensures that you will get more of the message. As much as 93 percent of the message the speaker will give you is nonverbal communication. You will need to see as well as hear what the speaker is saying.

Touch

Touch may not be appropriate in many settings, but when the speaker is someone close to you, touch can be very reassuring. Nonsexual touch—holding hands or sitting with your knees touching, hugs, pats on the back, a soft touch on the arm—can connect in the huge, nonverbal area of communication. Also, touch makes it more difficult to maintain anger. On occasion we have asked angry married partners to sit back to back, leaning against each other while they take turns talking and listening to one another. This can help break down some of the hostility they have been transmitting to each other nonverbally, while also connecting them emotionally and physically through touch.

Often Jesus used touch to communicate love and to administer healing. The apostle John, referring to himself as the disciple whom Jesus loved, "leaned on his breast at supper" (John 21:20; 21:4). Jesus touched little children in order to bless them. Ross Campbell speaks about how loving touch communicates far more powerfully than words to children.[22] They need loving touch in the same way that they need food. It nourishes them emotionally and can help to fill the attention deficit that so many children experience in our frantic, fast-paced world.

Encouraging Acknowledgments and Brief Expressions

The listener can encourage the speaker with occasional head nods and short, one- or two-word expressions like "Hum,"

"Uh-huh," "I see," "Right," or "Interesting." This tells the speaker that you are tracking with him.

Summarizing

The next skill in discovery listening is *summarizing*. Many authors have written and taught about this skill using labels such as reflective listening, active listening, paraphrasing, or mirroring. We have chosen to call it summarizing because this word captures the action of putting someone's message into your own words. We will show you what summarizing looks like and how to use it later in this chapter.

But first let's talk about some of the barriers people have to summarizing and why it is included in the discovery listening skill set. In the past, many have rejected summarizing as too psychological, too clinical, too unnatural, and too slow. From our experience, bright people find it extremely difficult to slow down enough to track with someone else. They may object to this part of the process and say, "Summarizing gets in the way." Others resist this portion because in the past, someone has used summarizing to wound or manipulate or control them. Finally the biggest obstacle to summarizing is that people find it too hard. It's easier to go back to the familiar ways, even though they have not been productive.

When we first learned how to summarize, we had some of these same objections. At first it sounded phony to us. We thought, *"People just don't talk this way."* Then as we began to encounter hardships in our own relationship, this summarizing skill increased in importance. More than any other part of the listening process, summarizing allowed us to connect across our differences. We can't imagine our marriage without this important listening skill. Like many couples, we are opposites in temperament, in gifting and aptitude, and in the way we think and express ourselves. Without summarizing placed in the hands of Christ in us, we couldn't live and work together today in the harmony and peace that prevails in our relationship. A major benefit of summarizing is that you see another's point of view. People have a different perspective based on their life experience. Summarizing helps you enter another's worldview, broaden your understanding, and enrich your own viewpoint.

"None of you should think only of his own affairs, but consider other people's interests too" (Phil. 2:4, PH).

Point of View

As an illustration of seeing things from other people's point of view, think about looking with someone at a painting or a new car, or discussing a subject like politics or religion. Almost anything you might consider with another person opens up the probability that you will have different points of view.

To illustrate this point further, think about looking at one of the great scenic wonders in the world such as the Grand Canyon. Suppose you and a friend decided to each view the canyon for the first time from its opposite sides. You go to the South Rim and your friend goes to the North Rim.

The North Rim is very different from the South Rim with its higher elevation, different vegetation, different weather, and fewer tourists. It's a different perspective.

When you got together to compare your vantage points, you would not argue over which one had the right view. You would accept that you saw the canyon from different perspectives.

Wait a minute, you may be thinking. *Aren't there black-and-white issues in which one person's viewpoint is clearly wrong?* Take for example moral issues condemned in the Bible. Perhaps a teenager is considering premarital sex because "all my friends are doing it," or a husband habitually visits porn sites on the Internet saying, "I'm not hurting anyone." Don't you have an obligation to speak up for what's right?

Understanding Doesn't Mean You Agree

We do have a responsibility to speak up for what's right. The question is how and when do we "speak up." If you will listen first so that you have a thorough understanding of the other person's position (as offensive as it may be), when it's your turn to talk your patient investment in understanding will "earn" you the right to be heard. In chapter 11 we talk further about how to invite someone to listen to you. Patiently listening is the first step.

Furthermore, listening to the other person first before giving your own point of view gives you an opportunity to show God's nature. Think about how He listens to you in kindness and great love, no matter what you do or say. The fact that He listens through the filter of His grace provides the greatest possible proof of His unconditional love. Likewise, as you listen to another person, you touch him at his greatest point of need. At the core of the other person's message, hidden beneath whatever façade or issue he presents, is almost always this question: *Do you really care?* Committed and patient focusing and summarizing transmits Christ's unconditional love straight to the heart of the other person's need. In a very real sense, listening is the greatest proof of God's presence loving through you.

Summarizing can also be extremely helpful when you are listening to someone who feels strongly about his or her point of view. "When feelings of not being understood come out in anger, sharing them, not shutting your ears or fighting back, is the key to calming things down."[23] As you summarize, you help the speaker bring his emotional level down so that he can effectively think through his problem.

Listening Quiz

Care to test your listening ability? Here are several situations with upset people. Choose the response you would most likely use.

Put yourself in the role of a pastor dealing with a disgruntled church member who comes to you and says, "I've been church organist in this church for over thirty years. Now the director of music has asked me to step down. After all these years of service, I feel like I'm being cast aside like an old shoe."

How would you respond?

☐ *"You should discuss your problems with the music director.
That's his area and I don't want to interfere."*

☐ *"When did he talk to you?"*

☐ *"Well, Mary, let's face it. Time marches on and we have to give
the younger ones a chance to serve, too."*

☐ *"You feel rejected and shoved aside as if you are no longer
appreciated or needed. You feel deeply hurt."*

☐ *"Nonsense, Mary, you've just been reassigned. God has something new for you to do. Have you ever thought about the children's department?"*

Here's another situation. Your spouse says, "Why don't you just
divorce me? I hardly see you any more. You're either at work or at
one of those church meetings. We see each other briefly before you
leave for work and maybe, if I'm lucky, before I go to bed."

How do you respond?

☐ *"Really, Hon, I think you're exaggerating. I was here last night
and where were you?"*

☐ *"Hang in there. This will be over when the church building cam-
paign is finished."*

☐ *"All I ever get from you is nag, nag, nag."*

☐ *"Sounds like you're missing me, and you're feeling lonely and
neglected. And fed up and angry. Is that right?"*

The summarizing responses are the empathetic-sounding ones
with "feeling" words in them: "Sounds like you're upset and worried" or "Sounds like you're missing me, and you're feeling lonely,
neglected, fed up, and angry." These nonjudgmental responses capture the essential theme or feeling expressed. They build rapport
and mutual understanding and they help to soothe the person
speaking to you.

*"Don't tell angry people to calm down. Doing so only makes them
feel that you're denying their right to be upset."*[24]

You may wonder if feelings are the only words you paraphrase.
Not always, but when people are upset and showing strong feelings,
those are most important words to summarize. When the person
hears you acknowledging his feelings, he will usually begin to feel

better. Like releasing the air out of balloon, the person lets go of some of the pressure and tension that go along with negative feelings. The fact that you hear him relieves his sense of being alone and perhaps misunderstood. Also, he gets a chance to hear himself and to take responsibility for his own thoughts, feelings, and behaviors.

Here are some other occasions when summarizing can help communication:

- *When you want to check your listening accuracy and encourage further discussion:* "Am I understanding you correctly?" ... then summarize.
- *When you want to pull the pieces of a discussion together:* "To summarize what you've said, these sound like the main points that concern you ..."

Here are some common communication pitfalls that summarizing helps you avoid:

- *Summarizing helps you avoid being critical and judgmental. A critical response is often perceived as persecution by others. They feel "put down" and "put off." Criticism invites them to react defensively and/or aggressively.*
- *Summarizing helps you avoid solving the speaker's problem and doing his thinking for him. Although solving the speaker's problem may make you feel important and powerful, it is done at the expense of the speaker's self-esteem. Culturally, we seem to think we're supposed to solve a problem when someone presents it to us. This is particularly true in the church. On the contrary, people feel encouraged and empowered when they can solve their own problems as they learn to draw on their own God-given resources.*

Keep in mind as you summarize that you don't have to agree with whatever someone says to you. In the next chapter, we will discuss how and when you might give your opposing viewpoint in a way that helps avoid a defensive reaction.

Now we're ready to look at how to summarize.

To summarize means to rephrase the speaker's message in your own words but *without adding your interpretation.*

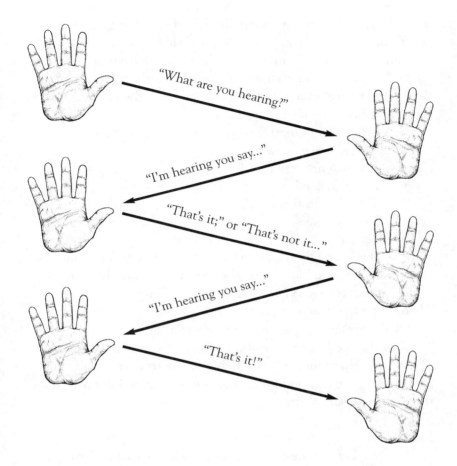

How to Summarize

At the beginning point in the diagram the speaker sends a message followed by the phrase, "What are you hearing?" The listener rephrases or summarizes the message in his own words beginning with the phrase, "I'm hearing you say ...." The speaker then accepts the summary: "That's it;" or clarifies it: "That's not it. Let me send the message again." The listener then restates the entire message, or the portion the listener summarized incorrectly. This process continues until the speaker says, "That's it. That's what I meant to say." The speaker is always the authority on his message.

In this diagram, we assume that the speaker is aware of the skill of summarizing and asks for it using the phrase, "What did you hear me say?" However, summarizing can be done with anyone at any time with or without the speaker being aware of the process. You can simply begin to summarize.

Here are some alternative ways to begin summarizing:

- *"You seem to be saying ..."*
- *"It sounds as if you're ..."*
- *"If I understand, you feel ..."*
- *"What I'm hearing is ..."*
- *"You want ..."*
- *"You feel ..."*

If the incoming message is getting too long for you to remember it all, hold your hand up to stop the speaker temporarily. Your job as the listener is to feed back the message in "bite-sized" pieces. Then invite the speaker to continue.

"Wait a minute, let me see if I've gotten this so far."

Now the speaker can confirm: "That's what I said;" or clarify: "That's not what I meant," in which case the speaker can send that part again, or he can simply continue on with more information for the listener to summarize.

Mutual Discovery

The purpose of summarizing is to increase mutual understanding and discovery. When you summarize, you are working to understand the words the speaker is sending your way. Your summary or restatement also allows the speaker to understand his own heart and mind. As he compares your restatement to what he intended to say, he gets another look at his own message. This helps him clarify and decode his message. In other words, speakers often do not understand themselves when they begin to speak. When you summarize, you make it safe for them to think out loud with you. You become an active partner with God in helping them discover their own mind and heart. Words are simply a code. A word merely represents the thing it names or describes.

The dictionary is full of thousands of words. However, most adults use only an average of five hundred of these words, and each word has between twenty and twenty-five meanings. This means any two people can use five hundred words with the possibility of 12,500 meanings.[25]

For example a speaker may use the word 'trunk', meaning a large suitcase, while the listener thinks of the trunk of a car. The simple statement, "My scarf is in the trunk. Will you go get it?" could result in an unnecessary trip to the car, unless the listener knows how to check out the meaning of the words. The meaning of the word is in the speaker. When the added ingredient of emotionally charged words is added, the importance of checking out your assumptions greatly multiplies. For example how many meanings could you think of for the word 'love'? Although it takes more time initially, checking out the meaning of the words the speaker uses saves time, energy, and resources in the long run. Checking out another person's meaning is as simple as saying, "Are you saying you want me to go get your scarf out of the trunk of the car?"

When you summarize the information, the speaker may clarify what you thought you heard. Don't let it upset you. The speaker has the right to do this, because it is *his* message you are trying to receive and understand. The speaker is the one who has authority over the message. It's his "work in process."

Any skill can seem mechanical at first because you aren't accustomed to it. But as you practice summarizing, you will find it as natural as breathing and with breathtaking results.

In the next chapter we will continue with the last two skills that make up the package of discovery listening skills.

Action Step: Listening Skills Practice

1. Invite someone to practice with you your new discovery listening skills. Tell and demonstrate with him what you want to integrate into your life.

2. Begin to notice your focusing behavior in conversations this week. What kinds of responses did you get when you practiced open posture, eye contact, head nods, and touch as you listened to others?

3. If you are in a small group, choose a partner and practice focusing while you talk about the "ups and downs" in your life this week.

4. How did people respond when you began to add summarizing as you listened to them?

5. In your small group, practice summarizing with a partner as you talk about this subject: "If there was one thing I'd like you to pray about for me this week, it would be ..."

Questions for Personal Reflection or Group Discussion

- *How did your parents' listening behaviors shape your life? How did they shape your ability to listen to others?*

- *Describe the ways you see yourself in the roles of rescuer, persecutor, or victim.*

7

Additional Steps for Discovery Listening

*"The greatest compliment that was ever paid me was when one
asked me what I thought, and attended to my answer."*
Henry David Thoreau[26]

Inviting

It's easy to learn the inviting step because it's only a couple
of words: "Say more" or "Is there more?" However, inviting a person
who is angry with you to say more may seem like sticking out your
chin and saying, "hit me." Even though it may seem foolish to
invite more angry words, the opposite is true. An invitation to continue, when used in tandem with the other listening skills, can help
to calm an angry person and to reduce the tension in a highly
charged emotional situation.

Let's return to Eric and Carol from the previous chapter. Carol was enraged at Eric. They had reached a point of crisis and Carol packed up the kids and went home to her parents' house. Eric came in for counseling alone because Carol had refused to come. In counseling he learned how to anchor in Christ and how to listen in a crisis situation.

After weeks of separation, Carol reluctantly agreed to come for a joint counseling session. Like releasing a fire hose, she poured out her angry feelings while Eric anchored himself in Christ and patiently focused and summarized. She began to soften toward him because he did not yell or leave the room as he always had before. As we join them, several minutes have passed and she hasn't said anything. He begins with an invitation:

"Is there more?" he asked, as he handed her another tissue.

"Yes," Carol said. "I don't really want to end our relationship. I never have."

He paused a moment, searching her face. "You don't want out of the marriage?" he said in an attempt to summarize.

"I didn't say that," she snapped. "Don't jump to conclusions! I said I didn't want to end the relationship. I'm just so frustrated and tired because nothing ever changes."

He summarized, "You're weary and frustrated because there's no apparent change."

"Yes," she answered. "I've tried everything ... seminars ... books ... telling you how I felt. But you just said I was the one who was unhappy so I needed to go get help."

A frown deepened the lines in his forehead, and his voice became almost a whisper.

"I blamed you and I took no part in the responsibility."

"That's it. You got it," she said.

He waited and when she remained silent, he asked, "Anything more?"

When to Invite

Typically the time to invite is when the speaker seems at a standstill. Maybe he hasn't spoken for a few seconds. Speakers can have many lulls like this before they find relief from some of their tangle. Just as you will have many opportunities to summarize, you may also use the skill of inviting many times before the speaker has said what he wants to say.

Why Invite More?

Your patient investment in inviting, used in tandem with the other listening skills, demonstrates God's love. As we have said before, giving the gift of listening gives you an opportunity to reveal God's nature living in you. Remember that at the core of the other person's message is almost always the plea "Do you really care?" Inviting, used in tandem with the other listening skills, penetrates to the heart of the other person's need. It affirms, "I do care." When you invite the other person to pour out more of his hurt and anger while you work to understand and validate his feelings, you demonstrate God's love reaching out through you.

You also demonstrate that you are anchored. Patient listening shows that your main source of peace, security, and love dwells within you. While you may desire the love and approval of the person speaking to you, you do not have a *desperate need* for their love. God has already filled that need as you choose to immerse yourself in the truth of His love for you.

Inviting helps the speaker move deeper into self-discovery. Like peeling the layers of an onion, your listening helps the speaker move closer and closer to the protected core of his message. This unspoken part may be something he is aware of and is wondering whether or not to reveal it to you, or it may be something below his awareness. He just needs your patient listening to prompt that something to bubble up to the surface. During these moments of discovery, the speaker may express surprise at what he heard himself say. He may say, "I never realized how I really felt before;" or "I've never told that to a living soul." We treat these as sacred moments. A time not to congratulate yourself for being a great listener, but to rejoice and thank God for what has just happened.

Reflect for a moment on what might have happened if you had

not invited the speaker to say more. Perhaps you decided you were tired of listening and that it was your turn to speak. You would have missed the privilege of seeing the breakthrough that the speaker needed to resolve his issue or to lower the level of tension in your relationship. You might have missed the opportunity to thank God for demonstrating His love both through your listening and the other person's courage to reveal his heart to you.

Now we come to the little finger and the last discovery listening skill, *asking*.

When to Ask

Wait until the speaker seems to have exhausted his supply of self-information. You have focused, summarized, and invited perhaps many times. He has indicated to you he is completely finished. Perhaps you have some questions. As the person talked, you noted a gap in the information. Often speakers leave out whole areas of important information. Through the use of a thoughtful question designed to access this hidden area, you can help them make further discoveries. At that point, you return to the other listening skill—focusing, summarizing, and inviting—to facilitate their exploration of the hidden area.

How to Begin

As you begin to ask questions, your first question may seem a bit strange or awkward at first. You ask: "Can I have permission to ask a question?" or "May I ask a question?"

Questions can seem like an invasion of privacy, or they can convey a lack of respect. For that reason, speakers sometimes get defensive when you ask questions. Asking permission to ask a question helps bypass that defensiveness.

Just as you would politely knock on a person's bedroom door and ask permission before entering, asking permission to ask a question politely "knocks" on the door of a person's heart territory. You are saying in effect, "May I come in?" If the speaker says "no" or "not right now," respect his need for privacy. Respecting the speaker's privacy helps deepen the trust in your relationship. However, if you have listened patiently and lovingly, the speaker will usually say, "Sure. What do you want to know?"

Let's continue the story of Eric and Carol to demonstrate the principle of asking.

"May I ask you a question?" he asked.

She nodded.

"You mentioned you were frustrated and angry when you left to go to your mother's. I'm wondering what else you were feeling?" he asked.

Carol paused for a moment looked at him. Then she said, "I thought you didn't care any more and I felt crushed. It was like you were behind a steel door and I could not get through."

He summarized, "You felt completely closed out. You thought I didn't care anymore and you were deeply hurt."

She nodded her head, her chin quivering.

After she reached for another tissue, Eric asked, "Is there more?"

Keep in mind these additional pointers about asking questions.

Use questions sparingly so the speaker doesn't feel as if he is getting the "third degree." After you ask the question, return to the other listening skills: focusing, summarizing, and inviting to help the speaker explore this new area.

Avoid asking "yes or no" questions because they give the speaker little leeway and can appear to be controlling. Open questions usually begin with the words "what" or "how." In the above illustration, Eric asked a great question: "What else were you feeling?" Almost every speaker can explore additional feelings. Other good questions are "What do you think?" "Can you give me a specific example?" and "What are you wanting?"

Avoid "why" questions because they tend to put the speaker on the defensive. For example, "Why do you say the things you do?" or "Why can't you stop doing that?" Most "why" questions can quickly undermine all your good effort and cause the speaker to shut down further communication.

How Does Discovery Listening Work?

Listening skills are helpful in many different types of situations including listening to your children. Here's a summary of every listening skill discussed to this point. This incident happened years ago soon after we began practicing discovery listening within our own family.

Kissing the Emotional "Owie"

When our daughter, Lori, was just beginning the stormy days of puberty, she came home from school one day and said, "I hate school. I'm never going back there again as long as I live."

In the past, I (Nancy) would have tried to talk Lori out of her feelings by saying things like "You don't really feel that way," or "It's not as bad as all that," or "Nonsense! Of course you're going to school!"

Instead, I decided to give Lori the gift of listening. At the very least, I thought this would be an opportunity to practice my new-found skill.

After sending up a quick prayer, "Lord, thank You that You live in me and therefore I have the patience and the ability to listen and not react." I sat down beside her at the kitchen table.

"So, school was really rough today?" I asked, looking into her tear-filled eyes.

"Yes," she said. "I hate school."

"School's awful," I said.

"Yes," she said, as her lips trembled and tears began to roll down her cheeks. "I'm never going back there. Please don't make me."

I reached out to hug her. "You can't imagine anything worse than going back to that school and you don't want me to make you go back."

"Yes," she said, sobbing. "I hate it. I hate it. I hate it!"

"You really hate it," I said. "You think it's the worst place in the world."

"Yes," she said.

"Is there more?" I asked.

"Are you gonna make me?" she asked.

"You're wondering if I'm going to make you go back?" I replied. She nodded.

"May I ask you a question?" I asked, avoiding her question.

"Yes," she said.

"What happened at school today?"

She went on to relate how the teacher corrected her "unjustly" in front of the class. How her attempts to defend herself were ignored. How she endured the jeers of some classmates.

As I continued to listen to her hurt, anger, and embarrassment, I extended love and comfort through touch, eye contact, summarizing, inviting, and asking well-timed questions. Her mood began to lift. Presently she asked for a snack and went out to play.

I was amazed. This new skill set felt like the healing balm I used when she was much younger. When she scraped a knee or skinned an elbow, she would run to my side and I would kiss her "owie." Through the skills of discovery listening, I could reach her emotional "owie." The next morning she went off to school without another word about her feelings from the day before or about "never going back."

Listening Is Fine, But When Can I Give Advice?

As you apply the discovery listening skill set, you will often feel as if you want to interrupt the listening process and tell the other person what to do to solve the problem.

For example, suppose you are listening to a young person who is considering having sex because "all my friends are doing it." Or in the story about Eric and Carol, what if you were listening to Carol who has left Eric and is wondering about divorce?

Critics of listening say, "How can you simply listen to someone when you know their thinking could lead them into a whole lot of trouble? As Christians, don't we have a responsibility to instruct and correct? If I'm going to exhibit Christian love, doesn't it also include exhortation and even confrontation?"

We respond with yes to each of these questions. At times, Christians do have a responsibility to correct and reprove, but the key is to know *when and how*. Most people move far too quickly into *telling* rather than *listening*. And when you tell another person rather than listen to him, you rob him of the joy of discovering his own God-given answers. You prevent him from strengthening his own confidence and connection with God. Besides, people are far more inclined to follow their own solutions than to heed someone else's advice. We seem to have a built-in resistance to someone else telling us what to do.

However, there are times when you have a responsibility to speak up. For that reason, we have added these cautions about when and how to give advice.

When and How to Give Advice

Advice should be given only as a last resort. Suppose you have already listened intensely and then asked skillful questions, yet the person still sounds as if he might "crash and burn" without more information. How do you give your opinion?

Ask Permission

First ask permission: "May I give an opinion?" This indicates you respect the person's right to say no. It also greatly reduces the person's resistance to considering your opinion.

After he agrees, share your advice. Start by asking, "Will you help me out?" Then ask the other person to rephrase or to summarize in his or her own words what you just said. Explain that this summary process will help you know if you said what you meant to say. You might then return to the listening role—to help him sort out what you just said to him.

It can't be emphasized enough that the need to give advice to the other person is more the exception than the rule. Normally the discovery listening skill set will help the speaker discover a solution as he talks through the various possibilities. You can best serve your colleague, your friend, your spouse, or your child as you exercise the gift of listening rather than give in to the temptation to "fix" them. As you practice these skills and anchor your heart and life in God's hands, you will be amazed at what will happen.

In the next chapter, you will journey into the ultimate listening experience—listening to God.

Questions for Personal Reflection or Group Discussion

- *Practice using all four skills with someone:* focusing, summarizing, inviting, *and* asking.

- *In a small group choose a partner and practice discovery listening using the question "If there is one thing I'd like prayer for this week, it is ..." Then change roles so that each person has a chance to practice listening skills.*

8

Listening to God

My sheep listen to my voice ...
John 10:27a

So far we have talked about how to listen to others. Now we will focus on the ultimate listening experience: listening to God. Pouring out your heart to God is a familiar experience to many Christians; however hearing from God may be another story.

When we talk to people about listening to God, they react in different ways. Some people express anxious concern. They wonder, *How will I know for sure that I'm hearing Him? What if it's just my own thoughts? Or what if it's Satan deceiving me?*

Others express shame. They say things like, "I pray to hear God as others seem to hear Him, but He never talks to me. What's wrong with me?"

Still others express sadness and longing. "I don't feel that close to God. I pray and I read my Bible, but He seems so far away."

In this chapter we will first examine why listening to God is crucial to your Christian life. Next we will look at several reasons you may not have entered into that wonderful experience. And finally, we will walk you step-by-step through an actual experience in listening to God.

Hearing God Is Important

Hearing God is an integral part of being anchored in Christ. Without it you can be at the mercy of your own unhealed, diseased thinking, or you can become dependent on others to hear God and interpret Him for you. But most of all, without hearing God you will miss out on an important aspect of a close, intimate, anchored relationship with Him. You may feel like the ragged, hungry, orphan child standing in the snow with your nose pressed against the restaurant window, watching laughing people eating wonderful food. You long to enter in, but you feel excluded, lonely, rejected, and starved.

Reasons People Don't Hear Him

One of the reasons people feel that they are "on the outside looking in" spiritually is because they have a wrong concept of God.

The Real God

A.W. Tozer wrote, "Nothing twists and deforms the soul more than a low or unworthy conception of God."[27]

David Ferguson makes the point that you can have an intimate love relationship only with the *real* God.[28] Jesus said, "Love the Lord your God with all your heart and with all your soul and with all your mind" (Matt. 22:37). But you and I can love only the real God.

Ferguson goes on to explain that you and I tend to see God as we experienced our own fathers. If our fathers were distant, demanding, demeaning, or disappointing, we tend to see God that way.

Eva, a soft-spoken and gentle seventy-year-old lady, came into my (Nancy's) counseling office. With shining eyes, she talked about her children, her husband, their lives, and their plans.

I listened, occasionally asking questions, drawing her out and enjoying her company. Eventually, she began to trust me with deeper things of the heart. Then her tears began to flow.

Eva's Story

I've never told a living soul what changed my relationship with my father. Up until I was eight or nine, I was the apple of my father's eye. I remember going everywhere with him, riding in his truck. When I was real little, I would stand on the seat beside him and he would shield me with his arm. I felt so safe.

Then he took my younger brother and me on a camping trip. I pretended to be the mother and boss around my brothers. When they complained to my dad, he got a funny look and suddenly became very quiet. Then he said, "Well, I guess we'll just have to leave her home after this."

And he did. In fact, after that Dad completely withdrew from me. I cried and cried and asked him to please tell my why, but he never did. I got the impression it was because I was female like my mother. He made it plain that he didn't like my mother.

Because of his rejection, I grew up believing something was wrong with me. I walked on eggshells trying to be good—trying so hard to win back his love—but he remained hardened toward me until the day he died.

When I asked Eva about her relationship with God, she sadly confessed she had always felt that God was far away, too. In fact she used some of the same words she had used to describe her relationship with her father: " I long to please Him, I try so hard, but I never measure up." Eva's God was cold and rejecting.

David Ferguson relates how his own father, who was a sergeant in the Marine Corps, conducted daily inspection of his room. One of the inspection rules was that there had to be two finger-widths between each clothes hanger in the closet, otherwise all the clothes came out onto the floor. For many years, David saw God in the same way—as a demanding and inspecting father.

Many Christians do not know the "real" God—the delighted God who welcomes the wayward son or daughter home with open arms and great joy. He's the God who fills and surrounds you with His Son. Could anyone but a delighted God want you so close? It's as if He has opened up His heart and placed you inside it.

The Real You

We have stated that we can love only the real God. But the verse "Love the Lord your God with all your heart and with all your soul and with all your mind" goes on to say, "Love your neighbor as yourself" (Matt. 22:39). Clearly the standard for loving others is your love for *yourself*. Yet many Christians do not love themselves. In fact, many hate themselves.

They hate the way they look.

They hate the way they feel.

They hate who they think they are.

We believe this is because most Christians do not know who they are—persons surrounded and filled with divine life. Unless you see yourself through the eyes of a God who delights in you, you will probably believe lies about yourself and therefore experience a negative flow of emotions toward yourself and toward others.

Who you are is not based on how you look, what others say about you, what you do, or what you feel about yourself. Who you are is based on who God says you are.

Here are a few verses among the many that tell you who God says you are.

"Holy"—not holier-than-thou or self-righteous, but purified, cleansed, forgiven—washed in His precious blood (Rom. 11:16; Eph. 1:4).

"joined to the Lord and one spirit with Him." His nature fills you—animating and energizing your life (1 Cor. 6:17).

"lavished with His love"—God is "in love" with you (1 John 3:1).

Experiencing God

Henry Blackaby in *Experiencing God* makes the astonishing statement that God is "pursuing relationship with you."[29]

The truth of God's pursuit of us can be traced through word pictures of the Bible describing our relationship with Him

" *friends with Christ*" (John 15:15)

"*children of God*" (John 1:12)

"*the bride of Christ*" (Rev. 19:7–8)

Each of the above descriptions adds to the truth of how much He cares for us, and yet each one is inadequate to reveal the whole truth about His love. The fact is God wants to be close to us:

closer than friend,

closer than a father to his child,

closer even than a bridegroom to his bride.

So God devised a way to merge with us—to get inside us—deeper than just under our skins or into our hearts, but into our spirits, our identities, the very essence of who we are.

"Christ in you, the hope of glory" (Col. 1:27b)

There are no words in human experience to describe this intimacy. Jesus said it this way several times in His last words to His disciples: "*On that day you will realize that I am in my Father, and you are in me, and I am in you*" (John 14:20).

Paul describes this relationship as so much more than a *changed* life. It's an *exchanged* life: "*I no longer live, but Christ lives in me*" (Gal. 2:20).

Christ lives in you, inside your unique packaging and personality. You are one spirit with Him, a partaker of His divine nature. We are not saying you *are* Christ or that you and I are "little Christs." We are saying that we are absorbed into the larger life of Christ.

When you know that you are surrounded and filled with a God who loves you and will never leave you, you then have a solid basis for a healthy self-image—not pride or arrogance, but a rock-solid confidence that you are loved and supernaturally equipped for loving others.

Love Your Neighbor as Yourself

We have said you can't love yourself until you know the real God. Only then can you see who you are from His perspective. Armed with that love and self-acceptance, you are then ready to love your neighbor. David and Teresa Ferguson make the point that your partnership, your union with God, makes it possible to love (and we would add *to listen to*) your nearest neighbor—the person or persons with whom you live, work, and worship.

Now we've come full circle back to the place where we began this chapter. We have said that you might not hear God because your concept of God is confused with how you saw your earthly father. We have also said that, based on your wrong concept of God, you may not know the real you. You may see yourself as someone unworthy of hearing God or relating to Him on an intimate basis. We have also said that both of these things—not knowing the real God or the real you—interfere with your relationships with others, including your ability to listen to them.

You Can Hear God

Hearing God comes as part of your "divine nature." You are "hardwired" for listening to the One who loves you.

"My sheep listen to my voice" (*John 10:27a*).

However, you may still question, *"How can I be sure that I'm hearing God and not myself—or worse yet—the Enemy?"* You may also think that you must hear an audible voice that sounds perhaps like Charleton Heston or James Earl Jones.

In the following exercise, adapted in part from the book *The Secret to the Christian Life* by Gene Edwards,[30] you will lay to rest both these concerns. First, you will pray Scripture and therefore know without a doubt that it is God speaking to you through His Word. Secondly, you will hear God speaking through your thoughts, not in an audible voice.

In our experience, this is how God usually speaks. Occasionally people relate that they heard an audible voice, but most of the time we hear Him through our thoughts.

Gene Edwards leads you into this experience with these words: *"You are about to enter into an ancient practice of the saints of all the centuries past, a practice and a heritage passed down through two millennia of the Christian faith. You are about to turn Scripture into prayer."*[31]

Start by getting alone with God. In our version of this exercise we ask you to use your listening skills. Begin with **Focusing**. Take a few minutes to get quiet and think about His love for you and yours for Him. Let all other distractions fall away. Take your time and don't feel that you have to rush this process.

Open your Bible to Psalm 23. Ask the Lord to speak to you out of the psalm. Then read Psalm 23:1 out loud to Him. It's okay if your mind becomes filled with other sights and impressions relating the verse to your own life. Continue to read and expand the verse as you "hear" more of what the Lord is speaking to you, based on your existing Bible understanding.

When there's lull in the flow of ideas, ask Him to "say more." (**Inviting**)

When questions arise, ask the Lord, *"What does this mean?"* or *"How does this apply to me?"* then summarize His answer. (**Asking** and **Summarizing**)

Let's look at just how this might sound:

Lord Jesus, I hear You saying You are my Shepherd. I shall not want. I am a lamb. I was made for a shepherd. I wasn't meant to have all the answers and to be strong and independent. You supply my needs. Thank You, Lord.

What else do You want to say? (**Inviting**)

I hear you say that you are a Good Shepherd. Trustworthy and pure in Your love and intentions toward me. That I can rest in Your arms.

You are a safe place. In fact, You are the only safe place in this life. Thank You, Jesus. (**Summarizing**)

Is there more? (**Inviting**)

Continue on in this way all through Psalm 23. Try to do all of Psalm 23 each day for a minimum of three mornings a week.

After you have spent time alone with Psalm 23, ask a partner to join you.

Your partner can learn from you how to share this experience with you. Most people catch on right away with a little instruction. You can do this together in person, over the telephone, or you can e-mail your responses back and forth.

Although this exercise can greatly enhance the intimacy in any of your relationships, we have discovered that many Christian couples—including ourselves for many years—shut off conversation with God from each other. How strange it seems that we could even share ourselves physically and yet remain apart spiritually—that we could maintain separate best-friend relationships with the same person (the Lord) and yet rarely have intimate conversation with Him in each other's company.

Perhaps this happens because couples don't know how to make the relationship with each other that "safe". Many shut down all avenues of intimacy—physical, emotional, and spiritual—because they feel they can't risk further hurt.

However, now that you know discovery listening skills, you can open up a powerful new pathway for intimacy with each other and with God.

When you meet together, use Psalm 23 the first time. After that select another Christ-centered passage—for example, sections out of Ephesians 1, Colossians 1, or John 14–17. The passages need not be over five to eight verses long.

Do not try to impress one another with your prayers. Be learners, not teachers. Allow the Holy Spirit to reveal what the Lord is saying to you personally as you proceed.

Before you start, decide who is taking the odd-numbered verses and who the even-numbered ones. One of you read verse one and turn it into a spoken paraphrase of the passage. The other takes verse two, etc. But each can add to the prayer of the other whenever something is sparked within your own spirit. Sometimes you may both end up praying something out of each other's verse.

At the end, sit quietly before the Lord and let Him love you deeply within your spirit.

Closing Prayer:

"Father, I'm so glad I can hear Your voice. Your nonjudgmental hearing and speaking powerfully draws me to You. Thank You that I no longer feel on the outside looking in. You continually speak to me and I hear Your words as echoes of the Scripture."

Questions for Personal Reflection or Group Discussion

* *If you had to choose one of the following descriptors of your dad, which one would it be: Distant, Demanding, Disappointed, or Delighted?*

* *How has your relationship with your father impacted your relationship with God?*

* *What do you think and feel about the Psalm 23 exercise? What questions or concerns do you have about it? If you were to persist in doing this, what difference could it make in your life?*

9

Discovery Talking:
How to Listen to Yourself

*If you don't listen to yourself,
it's unlikely that anyone else will.*
Michael Nichols[32]

Throughout this book, the skill of listening has been emphasized. With this chapter, the role emphasis changes to the person who is talking. Through the skills of discovery talking, you can understand yourself and stop the out-of-control downward spiral of your life. As you tap into self-understanding and the power of self-talk, you will be able to discern between fact and fantasy or between truth and deception.

As you improve your talking skills, you will increase your self-understanding and your ability to effectively verbalize your thoughts and feelings to another person.

Unclutter Your Mental Closet with Discovery Talking Skills[33]

Discovery talking skills help you to thoroughly formulate your thoughts and feelings and then fill in the holes in your communication. These skills help you unwrap the meaning of your thoughts so you can understand yourself and then effectively explain yourself to others when you desire.

Let's face it. Over the years, many words that are arranged in your mind as beliefs have been bottled up inside of you. These bottled words express feelings, events, strengths, desires, joys, defeats, hurts, and fears. All of these details from your past and present, when mixed with the circumstances you are currently facing, are the determining influences in the decisions you will make today.

For many, the problem is that they have not taken the time to investigate these details that comprise the person they really *are* and the things they really *want*. As a consequence, they may be at a loss to understand their behavior and the unfavorable reactions of others.

How many times have you faced a decision, but didn't know which way to turn? Through the use of discovery talking skills, you will uncover what you really desire in life and what motivates you in your particular issue. The journey inward is to find the mind of Christ, which is resident in you. Then as you look inward, you will also look upward in thanksgiving and praise to the One who is your life.

Those who trust God's action in them find that God's Spirit is in them—living and breathing God! ... Anyone completely absorbed in self ignores God, ends up thinking more about self than God. (See Romans 8, The Message.)

A wealth of valuable information lies buried in your heart. Discovery talking skills will serve as a map to help you, under the animation and direction of Christ, to organize your mental closet to find the buried information and clean out the clutter.

Create a Self-Discovery Map

To begin listening to yourself, consider a particular issue you want to work on—anything at all that concerns you.

Every idea—whether it is a thought, feeling, longing, action, or conflict—has a beginning point. It begins with an incident. Something happens that registers on the blank screen of your mind. The idea enters through the five senses—primarily through your eyes and ears—although smell, touch, and taste can be involved.

For example, Ruth—the wife of Gary, a businessman and leader of men's ministry in the church—was upset with her very busy husband. She had been distressed for some time, as she cycled and recycled anger, fear, and guilt about what was happening with Gary. In order to find relief, she took this inward journey by herself, and wrote down her answers to each part of the discovery talking process. She began asking herself, *What do I see and hear happening?*

SKILL ONE: WHAT I SEE AND HEAR

She wrote: "*I see myself cooking meals that aren't being eaten. Before dawn, I see Gary leaving the house and not returning home until after dark. I see myself sitting alone at home every evening. Even in church, I see myself alone because Gary leads the men's ministry on Sunday morning.*"

With this skill, notice that you are merely stating in a clear and concise manner the facts about what you see and hear. You haven't offered any interpretation about what you think the facts mean to you until you move on to the next skill.

SKILL TWO: WHAT I THINK

We use the word "think" to describe the process you go through in your mind to attach meaning to what you just saw and heard.

Once you receive information, your mind immediately goes to work making sense of it, forming an opinion or a conclusion based on the information that entered primarily through your eyes and ears.

You may jump to conclusions so rapidly that you are hardly aware that it happens. You make assumptions about what you saw and heard and then speculate about what something means. How do you know if your assumptions are right? Unless you ask the sender of the message "What does this mean?" you can't be certain about your assumptions. Many times, it's too late to ask because the event is long past. When it is in the past, all you can do is examine your assumptions and realize you might not have the whole picture.

Ruth writes: *What do I think? I think Gary is burning the candle at both ends. I think this men's ministry is crowding out my relationship with my husband. I think Gary's taking me for granted. I think he's inconsiderate of my needs. I think I'm not letting him in on my thoughts and feelings because he's doing "God's work." Also I think I'm trusting in him for my well being more than I am in the Lord.*

Ruth allows these random thoughts, which comprise the good and the-not-so-good, to spill out on paper. Now at this point in the discovery talking she is ready to enter the turbulent world of her feelings.

SKILL THREE: WHAT I FEEL

Feelings are not meant to be the primary movers of your life. As the freight cars follow the engine on a train, feelings follow your thoughts. If you let *feelings* lead you, instead of your *thinking*, you will be subject to the roller coaster of your moods. When your feelings lead you, then no doubt you will feel unstable and ungrounded.

On the other hand, without expression of feelings, you can seem uncaring and distant. Other people in your life have to guess about your feelings, which only adds to the confusion and miscommunication in your relationships. Expression of emotions is the centerpiece of intimacy. You cannot intimately know and be known outside of trusting others with some expression of your emotions.

Like thoughts, feelings can be formulated and stored before you even have a chance to bring them into your awareness. But be warned: *hidden feeling will eventually impact your outward behavior.* As a result, it's better to own your hidden feelings before they build up and leak out in destructive ways.

Expression of emotion, particularly long-held emotion, can cause you to feel vulnerable and anxious. You may think that others don't want to hear what you feel. You may not think you want to hear them yourself, as expressed in the following poem written by a participant in one of our seminars:

Feelings

Emotions in a box, neatly packed away
Nothing allowed to stick out or hang over the edge.
Don't be untidy!
If you can't store them neatly, at least keep the lid on.
Crying is for babies—babies are cute
and you can usually pacify them.
Find ways to soothe them.
Crying is not for you—it makes you unattractive.
Eyelids get puffy; nose becomes red and stuffy.
Sobbing is even worse.
Body shaking, rocking on waves of misery and pain.
Come on, get it in the box.
Get the lid down.
Hurry, hurry. Somebody is coming.
Draw down the curtains of your soul,
Pull up the corners of your mouth.
Ah, you are smiling now! Isn't that much better?
Inside you are dying, but that's okay,
At least you look normal.
We, the people, approve.

The recognition and expression of feelings is important for good mental and physical health. It provides a natural release of tension—far better than taking a pill or reaching for a substance to relieve stress. However, when painful feelings have been stuffed down inside you over time, they can hurt you in a number of ways. You no longer feel the good feelings like joy, peace, and love. In order to keep from feeling painful emotions, you may begin numbing out with addictive habits like overeating, using drugs or alcohol, viewing pornography, excessive shopping, overworking or overdoing good things like serving others in various forms of ministry.

However, just using the word "feeling" in your conversations does not necessarily mean you are expressing *emotions*.

"Feel That" Statements

When someone begins a statement saying, "I feel that ..." take note. This person isn't talking about a feeling. He is talking about a *thought* disguised as a feeling. Many people think they are talking about feelings and they continue to give "feel" statements. Because they aren't expressing true feelings, they aren't receiving the benefits of feeling expression, mentioned above.

The statement "I feel that you are not being totally honest with me" isn't a feeling; it's really a "think" statement. The true meaning of that previous sentence is "I *think* you are not being totally honest with me." To express the feeling, you would say, "And I *feel* anxious about it."

Or you can leave out the word "feeling" altogether and just label the emotion. For example, "I am angry," "I am worried," "I am scared," "I am confused." It is not necessary to use the word "feeling."

Primary Feelings

Because feelings are sometimes hard to find and for some people even harder to talk about, we've included four feeling categories to help you tap into your hidden emotions. Each category is vitally important. You may be unaware of one or two of them and fed up with others, but allow yourself to get in touch with each category. These types of feelings are most likely present in your personal or relationship conflicts, whether or not you are aware of them. To help you remember, we present them with the acronym SAGA— the "story" of your negative feelings.

S: sad
A: angry
G: guilty
A: afraid

Ruth, the distressed wife in our example, writes, "What do I feel?"

S: I'm *sad* and lonely. I miss him.

A: I'm *angry* that he's not thinking of my needs. I'm jealous of his ministry.

G: I'm feeling *guilty* about letting the "poor me" get the best of me. I'm ashamed because this is only a short window of time that I have to share him with this ministry and ashamed that I'm being such a high-maintenance wife.

A: I'm *afraid* he's not taking care of himself. I'm fearful of losing him.

These four feeling categories resemble primary colors. Just as all colors are a combination of the primary colors (red, yellow, and blue), every negative—and often hidden—feeling is constructed with combinations or variations of these four primary feelings. Notice how positive and negative feelings can coexist and yet conflict with each other—such as love and hate, or joy and sorrow.

Verbalizing the negative feelings either out loud or on paper is immensely helpful in resolving pain and confusion, and in uncovering the positive feelings that lie just beneath the surface.

Now you are ready for the next vital area. Once you receive information through eyes and ears, form conclusions about that information, and feel emotions in response—something else happens ...

SKILL FOUR: WHAT I WANT

Along with the jumble of the information that whirls inside your brain, you also experience *wants*. As a result of how you processed your information so far, you probably want to see several things happen—and some of these wants may conflict with each other, just as your feelings and your thinking sometimes are conflicted. If you aren't aware of the conflict, you may feel off in all directions or stuck and unable to act at all. To help clarify your wants, it will be important that you categorize them into four parts: what you want for *you*, what you want for the *other person(s)*, what you want for *both you and the other person(s)*, and what you want for God.

1. *What I want for me.*
2. *What I want for you.*
3. *What I want for us.*
4. *What I want for God.*

Notice that we didn't say what you want *from* someone else. What you want *for* a person differs greatly from you want *from* them. What you want from another is simply more of what you want for yourself. What you want for another helps you move your thoughts outward toward the welfare of others. What you want for God helps you focus the mind of Christ.

Your wants reveal the hidden motivations of your heart—the ones you like and the ones you don't like.

Ruth writes,

What I want for me:
- *I want revenge and to punish Gary.*
- *I want to hurt Gary,*
- *to control him,*
- *to get my needs met,*
- *to be heard,*
- *to be rid of these feelings,*
- *to be informed if he's missing dinner,*
- *to be reassured that I'm still loved,*
- *to be immersed in the Lord's love,*
- *and to forgive and release my husband to the Lord.*

What I want for him:
- *I want Gary to be free of distraction from a jealous, insecure wife,*
- *to be fulfilled and blessed by God,*
- *to experience his own consequences of not taking care of himself,*
- *to be free from a nagging wife.*

What I want for us:
- *I want to enjoy the time we have together,*
- *to use it to catch up on the events of each other's worlds,*
- *to have some fun together.*

What I want for God:

- I want God to enjoy my gratitude and adoration as I get my eyes off Gary and onto His grace and love,
- to enjoy my childlike dependence rather than fearful, complaining unbelief.

Notice how she looks at what she wants *for*, not *from*, God.

As she listened to her hidden motivations that were in conflict within, she realized why she had felt so upset and confused. She did not deny her negative feelings, but neither did she allow them to rule. And underneath the clutter of her self-centeredness, she found the treasure—thoughts, feelings, and wants—coming from her new nature in Christ.

Now she is ready to add a fifth question:

What's my plan of action? (As Ruth sorted through her motivations, she found a balanced and constructive plan of action, reflecting her new nature in Christ):

- turn to the Lord for comfort and love,
- forgive my husband,
- ask Gary to call me if he is coming home late,
- let Gary know that I am lonely and miss him,
- enjoy Gary when he can be with me.

The deeper you are willing to investigate the desires of your heart, the more you can apply the biblical principle of "taking every thought captive" (2 Cor. 10:3), which we will explore further in the next chapter. Your mind of Christ will pick up on those wants that are toxic and sinful. Rather than carry them and feel shame because of them, receive your forgiveness by faith. Christ died to give you freedom from condemnation. Thank Him for releasing you from the slave master of guilt and shame, and rejoice in the truth of your position in Christ.

"*Therefore, there is now no condemnation to those who are in Christ Jesus*" (Rom. 8:1).

Action Steps

Exercise One: Discovery Talking Skills—Listen to Your Self-Talk.
1. Create a "Discovery Map," as Ruth did, to help you resolve an issue. It could be a personal issue—one that goes on inside you and doesn't necessarily involve others. Or it could be a relationship issue—one that creates ongoing pain in your interaction with others.

Write:
- What I see and hear.
- What I think it means.
- What I feel.

Include SAGA—the "story" of my feelings. (Begin with the feeling uppermost on your mind.)

S. I'm sad about ...
A. I'm angry that ...
G. I'm guilty or ashamed about ...
A. I'm afraid of ...

Write:
- What I want:

Indicate what you want "for," not "from," others. What are the benefits you want for the other person(s)?
- For me:
- For other(s):
- For us:
- For God:

2. Amazing Questions for Listening to Yourself and to Others. Now you have a set of talking skills for self-discovery, but also you have a set of amazing questions to help you listen to yourself and to help other people listen to themselves. For this exercise, use these questions to help another person through an issue as you use discovery listening skills. These questions fit nicely into the asking part, or the little finger part, of discovery listening.

Here are the questions:
1. What do you see/hear?
2. What do you think?
3. What do you feel?
4. What are you sad about?
5. What are you angry about?
6. What are you feeling guilty or ashamed of?
7. What are you afraid of?
8. What do you want for yourself?
9. What do you want for another (others in the issue)?
10. What do you want for "us" collectively?
11. What do you want for God?
12. What plan of action do you see emerging?

10

Take Every Thought Captive
(2 Cor. 10:4–5)

Either we subjugate our thoughts to Christ,
or we are subjugated by them.
Leonard Sweet[34]

Lois held her head in her hands and moaned over and over, "Nobody cares. I've worked so hard. I've done my best, but it's not good enough. Why is God letting this happen? I just want to die."

For most of the hour, I (Nancy) listened to Lois, focusing, summarizing, inviting, and occasionally asking questions to help her clarify her thinking. I used discovery listening skills and then discovery talking skills as a template to help Lois clarify her own thoughts. Toward the end I asked to speak into her situation. With her permission, I began to remind Lois of who she is in Christ, bringing her back to the truth I had asked her to feed on—

transformational truth to build a solid self-image and help her respond to mental barrages—truth we had discussed several times before. As usual my words bounced off her mind like rain off an umbrella. Nothing seemed to be sinking in.

In contrast, I thought of Ken, another client whose life was equally in shambles during our first session together. However, Ken was able to receive the words. Like the seed that fell upon good soil in the Parable of the Sower, the same words Lois heard had taken root in Ken and *"produced a crop—a hundred, sixty, or thirty times what was sown. He who has ears, let him hear"* (Matt. 13:8–9). Within the first few weeks of counseling, Ken had devoured every book on our anchoring book list (Appendix A). Since the books pointed him to the Word of God, he began reading the Bible with great hunger. Now he is able to hear from God. His mental, emotional, and behavioral landscape was radically transformed. Ken went away with joy—thankful even for the sad events that he said "brought me to an end of myself."

Meanwhile I listened patiently to Lois and prayed that she would have an opening for a tiny seed of truth. I knew that, like a starving person, she could receive only a little nourishment at a time.

She needed crisis counseling and medical supervision immediately. But the listening skills in this book were useful to help her hear herself. As her story unfolded, I was able to ask questions like the ones from the last chapter to direct her into more self-understanding: *What do you see/hear? How did you interpret that experience? What do you feel? What do you want?*

As Lois answered the questions, I returned to focusing, summarizing, and inviting so she "heard" her answers and went deeper into exploring those areas. After I helped her sort and discover as much as possible from her own resources, I had a clear idea about some of the holes in her thinking. Then I asked her to listen to me as I slipped some of God's truth into the empty places in her storehouse of information.

Here are some basic facts from Lois' story, based on her answers to the discovery talking questions we covered in the last chapter.

What are past and present things she has seen and heard?

Lois' father was an alcoholic. For a stretch of time the family was homeless. Her family lived off welfare and the charity of others. Lois was a Christian. She graduated with honors from college and held two degrees. Currently she was raising three children alone because her husband had left her. She also lost her job.

What does Lois think about those events?

Even though Lois performed her way up the ladder of success, earning two college degrees and graduating with honors, she still thinks she is "less than" other people. Years of seeing herself as a second-class citizen or someone others don't respect had colored her thinking.

When she became a Christian, she intellectually believed God loved her, but His high value of her has not penetrated her toxic thoughts about herself. She thinks God loves her only if she performs for Him. And she measures her worth by how His people value her. Unfortunately she currently associates with Christian people who measure her worth based on how well she performs for them or how well she measures up to their Christian standards.

What does Lois feel in response to how she thinks?

S: She feels *sad* that she is always looked down on.

A: She feels *angry* with God, "Why does He keep letting this happen to me. I try my best to serve Him. What else does He want from me?"

G: She feels no *guilt* at this time. Right now she's blaming others and feeling a lot of self-pity.

A: She feels *afraid* of making friends and moving on in her life because people are always letting her down.

Lois feels fearful/angry/sad much of the time because of her mindset—because of the way she interprets information about herself from others and the way she interprets God in the light of how she viewed authority figures growing up. Her heart was full of judgment and she was seething with anger. The events that brought

her into counseling—her husband leaving and the loss of her job—
served only to expose what was already present: a negative self-image
and a victim mentality.

What does Lois *want*, in light of how she interprets and feels
about what has happened to her?

When we began counseling, Lois blamed others, including God,
and demanded that people change to meet her needs. Her worth was
based on what she thought others thought of her, which meant she
was worthless and worthy of rejection. Thinking others rejected her,
she felt anger and resentment toward them. Consequently, she
effused hostility—and others then did reject her. Thus, she pushed
away the love she craved and reinforced her negative self-image.

Like many Christians, Lois was on a performance treadmill—
working as hard as she could, but never arriving—growing more and
more defeated everyday. Her destructive thinking deflected the grace
of God from healing and transforming her identity.

Lois viewed a negative event as part of a never-ending pattern of
defeat. She moaned, "This always happens to me." She was supercrit-
ical of herself and of others, reflected in the *should's*, *ought's*, and
have-to's that spilled out as she talked in judgment of herself and
others. She placed a negative mental filter over everything in her
life, thereby excluding God's truth about her. She was adamant that
her accomplishments and positive qualities didn't count. Here are
some of her destructive thinking habits.

Toxic Thinking Patterns[35]

Mind Reading. When you assume what someone else is thinking
and feeling, it's called mind reading. Lois took ownership of others'
thoughts, feelings, and wants as if she could read their minds. Then
she reacted to her own fantasy, believing it was true.

All-or-nothing thinking. Lois saw events in her life in black-or-
white categories. When a situation didn't turn out as she expected or
wanted, it was a total failure. She was a total failure.

Overgeneralization. She saw a single negative event, such as her husband leaving, as a never-ending pattern of defeat. She used words such as "always" or "never" when she thought about it: "This kind of thing always happens to me."

Magnification. She exaggerated the importance of her problems and minimized her desirable qualities.

Emotional reasoning. She assumed that her negative emotions reflected reality: "Life is not worth living."

"Should" statements. She told herself that things should be the way she wanted them. "He shouldn't treat me this way." "They shouldn't have fired me." "God shouldn't allow things like this to happen." The *shoulds* directed toward others led Lois into ongoing anger and frustration. In Lois' case, her *shoulds* toward herself reflected a deep, abiding shame about who she was as a person. Guilt could be confessed and removed by repentance. But shame lingered on in spite of the confession because it was all tied up with her destructive self-image.

Labeling. She labeled herself: "I'm just a woman. "I'm just a loser." "I'm fat." "I'm ugly." Labeling is an assumption that you are the same as what you do, what you think, what you look like, and what you feel. It leads to more anger, frustration, hatred, fear, anxiety, sadness, and low self-esteem.

Blame. She blamed others for her problems. "He's such a jerk." "They are miserable excuses as Christians." She overlooked how she might be contributing to the problem. This blame kept her stuck in destructive *reacting*, rather than *resolving* the issues.

"Thoughts are missiles you can hurl from your head that can help or hurt others."

Helping Lois Hear Her Own Toxic Thoughts

Listen in on the end of one of our first sessions together. I had heard her long, dismal story that seemed so hopeless in light of her mind-set.

"Lois, may I ask you a question?" I asked.

She nodded, staring blankly at me.

"What are you thinking?" I asked.

"I'm thinking my life is over. There's no point in going on," she said, looking at the floor.

"So, you're thinking that you might as well end it all. There's no reason you can think of to continue," I said, feeling my muscles tense and praying, *Oh, Lord, thank You that You are here, and thank You for taking the weight of what I'm hearing from my shoulders.*

"Is there more?" I asked.

She thought a moment then said, "I guess, the only reason to continue would be for my kids."

"You're thinking now that being here for your children is a reason for living."

"Yes, that and I can't stand the thought of my ex-husband raising them," Lois said.

"So part of you wants to avoid leaving them for your ex-husband to raise."

"Yes," she said laughing.

"Can I ask you another question?" I said, smiling along with her.

"Sure," Lois said.

"What are you feeling right now?"

"I'm feeling good right now," she said. "I guess being so angry at him has its positive side." She laughed again.

This little slice of dialogue from our session shows how listening helps lighten the load. Lois had talked about a lot of sad things, and the talk about suicide was hard to hear. But as I listened and helped her sort out the feelings, she experienced relief.

As I entered her dark world to listen, I carefully anchored myself in Christ. Her burden was heavy and I must not carry it, except to the cross. My prayer was that soon Lois would be able to leave her burden there also.

Detoxifying Thoughts

As I wrote this chapter, Lois had already taken a major step away from her toxic thinking and she reaped the rewards. One of her first steps in this direction was to compare her distorted thinking with what God says about her. She needed to stop the flow of toxic thoughts with truth through the process Paul described as "taking thoughts captive" (2 Cor. 10:4).

Lois needed to replace the old diseased thinking with the truth of God's Word. As her homework assignment, I asked her to read books rich in truth from the anchoring booklist (Appendix A) about the grace of God. These books told Lois that she isn't a worthless person but rather someone who is one spirit with Christ.

I gave her a list of Scriptures to look up, then asked her to write in a journal. These Scriptures, which you will find in the Action Steps at the end of this chapter, contain powerful transformational truth about who Lois is and how God feels about her—Scriptures such as the following passage from the mouth of Jesus.

Come to me all you who are weary and burdened, and I will give you rest. Take my yoke upon you and learn from me, for I am gentle and humble in heart, and you will find rest for your souls (Mark 11:28, 29).

Lois learned that God wanted to get close to her—not to hurt her as her alcoholic father or her ex-husband did, but to love her.

This picture of God was radically different from her earthly father. The Lord God is gentle and humble in heart, and He gives rest as she begins to replace toxic thoughts with transformational truth. His love and His rest are not given because she earned them, but simply because she belongs to Christ.

Lois was beginning to understand that the Deceiver used her destructive thought patterns to condemn her, in spite of the fact that there was no condemnation for *"those who are in Christ Jesus"* (*Rom. 8:1*). As she recognized the lies and diseased thinking coming at her, she learned to stop these lies with the truth.

As Lois meditated on the identity verses in her journal and listened to God in the manner we discussed in chapter 8, she literally reprogrammed her mind under the power and direction of the Holy Spirit.

Now, using the discovery talking skills format, Lois has worked through her issues while "taking thoughts captive."

Taking Thoughts Captive Using Discovery Talking Skills

Here's how Lois and I worked through one strand of her tangled "low self-esteem" knot using her newfound ability to take thoughts captive.

WHAT DO I SEE/HEAR?

Lois visited a friend who served their lunch on paper plates. During their conversation her friend mentioned, "I'm going to be using my best china at a dinner party for some friends from church."

WHAT DO I THINK?

The thought comes at Lois' mind like a meteor hurtling to earth, *My friend doesn't value me. She uses paper plates for me then flaunts the planning of a dinner party using her best china and I'm not even invited.* But instead of receiving the thought, she exploded it in midair with the truth. *Thank You, Lord, that I cannot be rejected. You have given me Your life in exchange for mine. I am one with You and the Father. I choose to believe my worth is based on what You say about me and what You feel about me. My worth is not based on what I think others may think or say about me.*

WHAT DO I FEEL?

Lois' feelings followed right behind her thinking, like obedient children. In response to the powerful thoughts above, she began to feel joy and peace. She began to feel a measure of respect and love toward herself; whereas if she had entertained the toxic thought, she could have easily slipped back under the black cloud of despair.

WHAT DO I WANT?

It no longer mattered whether her friend was disrespectful or not. She wanted to enjoy the thought that Christ died for the love of her. She found herself wanting to extend love and forgiveness to her friend just as Christ extended love and forgiveness to her.

Lois' whole mental and emotional landscape is hanging together because she chooses to focus on transformational truth about herself more of the time.

Is this just an exercise in positive thinking? A matter of willpower? Or is Lois employing spiritual power against forces of spiritual darkness? Listen as the Scripture passage on "taking thoughts captive" continues:

"The weapons we fight with are not the weapons of the world. On the contrary, they have divine power to demolish strongholds." Paul goes on to explain what strongholds are. *"We demolish arguments and every pretension that sets itself up against the knowledge of God, and we take captive every thought to make it obedient to Christ"* (2 Cor. 10:5–6).

Taking thoughts captive sounds like military language—warfare, to be exact. And that's just what it is. Satan doesn't want you to live by God's truths. Why? Because these powerful thoughts will bring peace and joy to your mind and your relationships. Satan's goal is to stop your effectiveness as a Christian in any way possible. If you aren't aware of his game plan, he can convince you of anything. Using first-person pronouns so that it sounds like your thinking, Satan can continue to input lies about you, your spouse, or anyone else in your life—twisting and jerking you around according to his disruptive plan for your life.

Therefore, using your ability in Christ to prevent condemning thoughts about you and others (or any of a host of habitual destructive thought patterns) becomes central to your success in the Christian life.

WHAT ARE YOU THINKING?

You can begin taking thoughts captive as you become *aware* of what you hear in your head about yourself—thoughts that contradict the truth about who you are in Christ.

We ask people to begin writing down the thoughts they are constantly hearing in their minds that result in fear, anger, sadness, shame, and conflict with others. Why? Because these are often the thoughts that contradict what God says about them and about others. They believe these thoughts because they have become part of the person's belief system—no longer examined or questioned.

When we ask people to write out these condemning thoughts in order to become aware of them, we also ask them to write down the truth—what Scripture says in light of their new identity in Christ, in contrast to what they have been hearing. There is enough truth in the identity Scriptures at the end of this chapter to revolutionize your thinking. The book list we have included in the appendix will give you an expanding source of new Scripture to capture in your journal for further meditation and dialogue with God.

Changing the programs in your computer-brain to line up with what God says about you requires new input into your memory banks—input that contradicts the lies deeply embedded in your thoughts about who you are.

"Cognitive theorists tell us you and I generate 60,000 thoughts a day. This translates into a thought for every 1.44 seconds. Thoughts that may be true or false, noble or debased, just or unjust, pure or impure, loving or spiteful."[36]

Thoughts are powerful determinants of behavior. You will "life out" what you believe is true about you. Intentionally "feasting your mind" on the passages that tell you who you are in Christ and choosing to believe them will drastically change your attitude about yourself and your relationships with others.

"Be transformed by the renewing of your mind"
(Romans 12:1).

"What is the primary word God sends to you? Jesus. He radiates Him into your being or the mystery of Christ in you. It's a personal word. This loving, powerful, intimate word penetrates not only sense, eyes, nose, touch, smell and taste but the essence of your identity—who you are."[37]

You will be amazed at the difference in how you feel when you learn to stop the accusing, condemning thoughts about yourself and others. Changing your thoughts, or in other words, "reprogramming your computer (brain) will mean the difference between days of despair and days of peace and confidence, the difference between relationships that have simply existed for years and ones that exude the love of Christ."[38]

As you practice tuning in to the negative flow, replace it with the truth of what God thinks about you. The emotional climate of your life will change drastically as you begin to rest in the wonder of His acceptance and his love.

Action Steps

1. Look up this list of Scriptures and write them out using the first-person singular pronoun "I". For example, *In Christ I am ...* Matt. 5:14; 2 Cor. 5:17–18; Eph. 1:1; Eph. 6:2; Eph. 2:10; Phil. 3:20; John 15:15; 1 Cor. 6:17; 1 Cor. 6:20; 2 Cor. 5:21; Eph. 1:5; Eph. 2:18; Eph. 3:12; Col. 2:10; John 1:12; Rom. 8:28; Rom. 8:35; 2 Cor. 1:21; Col. 1:13; Phil. 4:13; 2 Tim. 1:7; Heb. 4:16; 1 John 5:18; 1 Cor. 6:17; 2 Peter 1:4; 1 Cor. 2:16; Rom. 5:17.

2. Here's an exercise in "taking thoughts captive." Divide a piece of paper into two columns. In one column, write out your negative thoughts and thought patterns of the day—thoughts that contradict who you or others are in Christ. Then listen to the word God is speaking to you, perhaps from the above verses. In the second column write words from Him that replace the negative, diseased patterns of thought.

3. Using the discovery talking skills format, take one strand of negative thinking and process it through the four questions: What do I see/hear? What do I think? What do I feel? What do I want for me, for others, for God?

11

Inviting Others to Listen to You

*Most people will not really listen or pay attention to
your point of view until they become convinced you
have heard and appreciate theirs.*
Michael Nichols

When do you invite others to listen to your heart? Whom
do you invite? These aspects are important for effective listening.
In previous chapters we have shown how active participation in listening to yourself, to God, and to others opens powerful pathways
for healing. We have also shown how God's grace can flow on this
pathway, enriching your life and the lives of others.

In this chapter the healing flow continues and your role
changes from a listener to a speaker. Now you learn how to invite
others to listen to you. Because you are giving others the gift of
listening, it's good to know you've already gained the ear of another
person. You have a place to begin inviting others to listen to you.

Give the Gift of Listening

Your investment in listening to the speaker has helped create a readiness, perhaps even an eagerness, to hear what you have to say. A key benefit of listening is building trust, safety, and connection. It opens up a bridge for two-way communication. Listening in its purest form is giving the gift of love.

Even when your listening has motivated another person to now listen to you, you can quickly demotivate this eager listener through your words and actions if you are not careful. What a shame if after your unselfish investment in listening to another person, you blow it when it is your turn to speak.

"A gentle answer turns away wrath, but a harsh word stirs up anger" (Prov. 15:1).

Know What Your Body Is Saying

First consider how your nonverbal behavior impacts the listener. Chapter 6 dealt with nonverbal communication when you were thinking about your role as a listener. How do you as a speaker impact the listener nonverbally?

A middle-level manager, Michael, told this example of how his nonverbal behavior affected a colleague at work. Michael sensed something wasn't going well between them, so he went to Peter, his colleague, and asked him for some feedback.

Because he invited feedback, Michael listened to Peter say, "Whenever I come to you with an issue, you frown while you listen and while you talk to me. In addition, you fold your arms across your chest, which makes you seem even more defensive and closed off. This makes it hard for me to listen to you when it's your turn to speak."

Later Michael reflected, "I had no idea that I was frowning and folding my arms in a way that seemed disapproving and critical while Peter talked to me. I was busy thinking about how I should solve the issue he was talking about. I can sure understand why he reacted the way he did."

"Instruct a wise man and he will be wiser still ..." (Proverbs 9:9a).

Some of the other behaviors that are frequently interpreted as critical or angry include rolling your eyes, narrowing your eyes, having rigid body posture, scowling, or shaking your finger. Silence can also be interpreted as anger or boredom if you also appear to disconnect from the listener by staring off into space, eyes almost unblinking, with perhaps a glazed look. Also impatient body movements—such a nervous swinging of a foot, frequent weight shifts while either standing or sitting, or finger drumming—can be interpreted as signs of boredom or impatience. Tuning into your nonverbal behavior will help others listen to you.

Much of our nonverbal behavior stems from internal tension that is below awareness. How can you change a behavior if you aren't aware of the cause of that behavior?

For example, when Michael in the above illustration tuned in to his emotions, he identified fear as the most pronounced feeling whenever he talked with anyone in equal or higher status or authority. He was anxious about how he was coming across, just as he had been as a child talking to his very strict and critical father.

Get Anchored

Your nonverbal behaviors stem from your underlying attitude and emotion. With each exchange with another person, you reflect your attitude toward God, yourself, and the other person. Your question may be at this point, *How can I change a behavior if I don't know what's causing it? Or even that I'm doing it?*

The answer leads us back to anchoring. When you choose to believe what God says about you, you begin to feel secure. Out of God's unconditional love you have a solid basis for accepting and caring for yourself. This self-acceptance isn't based on your performance, but on the fact that God loves you and has made His home in you.

"Don't you know that you yourselves are God's temple and that God's Spirit lives in you?" (1 Cor. 3:16).

As you rest in this security, you can extend an attitude of genuine love toward others—even people with whom you don't have a natural caring or affinity. This acceptance of people is not based on their performance or your attraction or positive feeling toward them. It's based on the fact of God's love for you and your availability to allow Him to love through you.

When your attitude comes from Jesus, your words and your behavior will be in harmony and you won't have to monitor the nonverbal message from your body. Instead your face and your body will radiate the genuine peace you're feeling on the inside.

Speak for Yourself

Some people struggle to use the pronoun "I" in their speaking. To reveal yourself with "I" statements can seem risky, unsafe, and even foolhardy. These feelings are especially true if you are uneasy about your own identity.

Possibly you've disguised yourself with a false identity like the "Super Me" described in the poem below written by a dear lady who attended our seminar.

Demise of a Perfectionist
Super Me is dead
Defeated on the Cross 2,000 years ago
But her crafty manners had me so fooled and faked out
That I thought she was still around.
Oh, how I battled with her false claims upon my life,
Forever trying to make me a showcase.
For she knew all the "should haves" and the "ought tos."
A ghostly cattle prod she was.
But why waste time on her obituary?
Rather welcome the Real Me,
Still a baby needing the milk of God's Word
But quickly growing into a child.
Learning to walk in His ways,
Stumbling at times,
Falling all the way at others.
Yet always seeking the Father's hand as

He reaches for her to pick her up,
To brush off the dirt and the dust of this world.
He carries her in His arms, dandles her upon His knee,
And reminds her that He loves her as she is
And that one day she will be like Him.

L. Nagel

For you to use the pronoun "I" can be an act of courage. Numerous times in Romans 7, the apostle Paul uses the pronoun "I" to separate the real self from the "phony" or "fleshly" self, which is fueled from sin's power. The word "you" coupled with "should," "ought," "can't," "always," or "never" sounds controlling, legalistic, demanding, and superior whether you are referring to yourself or to someone else. Remember: a primary goal of the gift of listening is the creation of a safe place where heart-to-heart dialogue can take place. "You" messages, especially when followed by the words "should," "can't," "ought," "always," or "never" can make communication feel very unsafe.

Therefore, knowing how to substitute "I" messages for "you" messages can prevent and resolve much misunderstanding and conflict in your relationships. When you know and receive God's grace, it can rid you of "should" messages about yourself and others.

What does an "I" message sound like?

"I heard the door slam." "I'm scared." "I'm confused." "I'm worried you might not change." "I think you're unhappy with me a lot of the time." "I'm hurt and disappointed about what's happened."

Contrast these statements with "You" messages: "You slammed the door." "You are scaring me." "You're making me confused." "You'll never change." "You're always on my case." "You're always hurting me and letting me down." "You make me angry."

"You" messages claim ownership over someone else's thoughts and feelings. These words imply that you are a victim without power or control over your own emotions. Also you place the responsibility for your choices and reactions on the other person.

This victim mentality not only adds to your sense of being "stuck," but it invites a defensive reaction from others. Truly, nobody makes you mad, sad, or glad. You choose how you will react.

To take responsibility for your own feelings and reactions, change the statement to "I'm _____ (fill in the blank with *angry, sad, mad*) about" and describe the behavior that bothers you.

When do you use "you" statements?

Are "you" statements ever appropriate? Yes, it is acceptable to use "you" statements when you are the teacher or leader. However, if your role as the leader, teacher, or authority is unclear or unwelcome, then tension and relational distance can quickly develop when you use "you" messages.

Finally, when you speak, avoid using "we" statements such as: "We're not hungry" or "We would be glad to come." A possible exception would be if you have checked with your partner or others in your group before you make the statement. If you speak for another person without his permission or agreement, then "we" statements sound controlling and invite a reaction of defensiveness and anger.

Because you are prepared to speak self-responsibly with "I" statements, you are ready to launch into greater depths for your speaking.

Invite the other person to listen to you

When you have listened well to someone's point of view, you have in a sense earned the right to be heard. Ask the person, "Would you now be willing to help me sort out my thoughts as you summarize what I'm attempting to say?"

If you humbly ask for help because of your need to express yourself clearly and nonjudgmentally, others are likely to accommodate you. Your unassuming attitude is extremely important here, or else the other person might think you are "parenting" him or implying that he isn't listening to you.

Know What You Want to Say by Using Discovery Talking Skills

It helps to have the objective of your message and your information clear before you begin. One way to do that is to use the discovery talking skills "hand" diagram to work through your message in advance, just as you did in chapter 9 (Discovery Talking Skills—Listening to Yourself).

Or you can follow the discovery talking format as an outline in your head as you spontaneously work through an issue with another person.

Each skill is useful when used alone or in combination with one another. The next five points cover these discovery talking skills.

1. Checking out with an "I see/hear" statement: Seeing her husband walk inside the house from work, she notices he isn't smiling, his eyes are downcast, his jaw is set, and his only response is a grunt in response to her "Hi, honey."

She doesn't jump to conclusions or accuse him by saying something like "What are you mad about now!" Nor does she withdraw in confusion, fear or anger. Rather she says, "I noticed your head down when you came in tonight, and I didn't hear you say anything when I said, 'Hi.'" She follows her observation with a "checking out" statement: "… and I wonder what might be happening with you?"

Notice the tentative nature of her statement, "I wonder." Through the use of this phrase, she acknowledges she can only speculate on the meaning of his behavior. He is the authority for his own message.

Her description of what she sees and hears and her request for his explanation serve as an invitation, not a demand, for him to communicate.

2. Make a "think" statement: She could also make an "I think" statement in combination with an "I see/I hear" statement such as "I noticed your head down, and you didn't respond when I spoke to you. My first thought was, 'He is mad at me.' Then I thought, 'Did something happen at work?'" Then she could follow with a checking-out question. "… and I'm wondering what, if anything, is going on with you?"

3. Make a "feeling" statement: She adds a feeling statement in combination with the others. Notice that each one builds on the next. "I notice you aren't smiling. I saw your eyes looking down at the ground and I didn't hear you say anything. In addition to wondering if you are mad at me, I'm feeling anxious and a bit annoyed about your silence." (Notice that you can have two or more emotional responses to the same stimulus.) Again, she could follow with a checking-out question: "What's happening?"

4. Make a "wanting" statement: If she makes the choice to be wide open and vulnerable with him, she could also add some wanting statements in addition to the other skills.

A want for herself is "I want to know what is bothering you, if anything, so I won't feel so anxious."

A want for her husband is "I want you to get relief from whatever might be bothering you."

A want for the two of them is "I want us to have a pleasant evening together."

5. Ask for summary: Each of these previous suggestions for helping others listen to you and to enable you to send clear messages will enhance your communication. However, unless the listener summarizes what you said, you have no way of knowing what he understood. If you say something you really want the listener to understand, ask him to summarize your words. This exchange greatly increases listening accuracy. At first it seems awkward to ask for a summary. "What did you hear me say?" can come across as parenting when the question is tacked onto the end of a message. It also can sound like a teacher who springs a "pop quiz" on the listener. The best way to defuse this type of reaction is to tell the listener *before* you begin the message that you need his assistance. Most people respond to a sincere request for help. You can say something like "I need your help. I have something to say, but I'm not sure if I'll say it the way I want to. Will you help me by putting it in your own words?"

A Two-Way Bridge

Summarizing not only helps the listener understand you, it will clarify your own message. You may not have selected a good "code" to express what you wanted to say. When you ask for a summary, it helps you sort out your own message in case you didn't say it right the first time. You are enlisting the listener to provide for you what you just did for him. You are helping the other person make it safe for you so you can open your heart and make discoveries.

Through this process, your bridge from listening to another person has become a two-way connection. This effort to construct a two-way bridge works well, not only for one-on-one communication, but can also be valuable for small or large groups. In our seminars, we model these skills with groups of several hundred.

Large-Group Interaction

In a large group setting, we speak for a short span of time such as ten minutes. Then we ask the crowd for a summary. We walk into the crowd with a hand microphone and ask questions such as:

- *"What did you hear us say that grabbed you?"*
- *"What didn't we say that leaves you with questions or concerns?"*
- *"If this were so, what difference could it make in your life?"*

After their comments we model the listening skills.

- *"So what you're saying is that ..."*
- *"Could you say more about that?"*
- *"Can I ask you a question about that?"*
- *"I'm wondering if I could make a comment about what I'm hearing you say?"*

From this process, we've discovered the audience learns as much, if not more, from what *they* say as from what we say. And the dialogue makes the audience an active participant as they tell their stories, get their objections into the open so that walls of misunderstanding and resistance come down, invite laughter and sometimes tears as people open their hearts with us and with each other.

The open sharing and risk taking is electrifying as people remove their masks and get to know each other. We do this for maybe five or ten minutes, then we go back to speaking from our notes or spontaneously on the spin-offs from the dialogue.

It's exciting for us to observe pastors and teachers as they adopt this interactive process. In our experience, people learn far more from interaction than they do from passively listening to a speaker. And they also get relationally connected with each other even in a large group setting.

Action Steps

Pick a subject to practice the skills. If you are reading this material with someone else or a small group, choose an issue that concerns each of you.

- *It could be a challenge you are facing at home or on the job ...*
- *It might be a pattern of behavior that you are exhibiting, but you don't understand why ...*
- *Perhaps you are in the midst of a decision, and you need to understand more about which direction you should go ...*
- *Or maybe you had a recent disagreement with someone ...*

The discovery talking skills will help you sort out the thoughts, experiences, and emotions that are stored in your heart around a specific subject of concern or interest as the other person assists you through the use of discovery listening skills.

Be sure to then change roles so that each of you has a turn using both skill sets.

12

How One Couple Put It All Together

Maybe you won't get through to the other person as long as you keep approaching him the same way you always do.
Michael Nichols[39]

At 1:40 on a gray afternoon, Debbie and Bill met in a restaurant for coffee. They sat in a corner booth near a window facing the street. Bill watched the people hurry past in the mid-November chill as he inwardly asked himself a string of familiar questions: *What did I say to her this time? She keeps saying it isn't what I say, but how I'm saying it ... well just how do I say it? It seems no matter what I say or do, she's never satisfied.*

On the other side of the table, Debbie stared into her steaming mug. Nine years of pain were flooding through her mind. She thought to herself, *It's like we're speaking two different languages. We talk, but we don't understand ... and the more we talk, the more frustrated we get. All I know is I'm tired of the fighting and the loneliness and the guilt ... and I'm tired of trying one more time and getting hurt all over again.*

Bill set his cup down and leaned toward her—his hands spread, his palms open, his eyes searching hers. "Deb, I don't know who's right and who's wrong in this situation. I know that much of the time, it's me. I admit I've been hardhearted and stubborn. But please don't give up on us. We can find a way to work this out— I know we can."

She held his gaze a long time, as if measuring him with some yardstick she carried. Finally, she stood. "I can't handle this any longer," she said and walked away.

Reconnecting

Three weeks later they sat in front of us in our counseling office. Anger still sparked in Debbie's eyes. Fear and hopelessness lined Bill's face. Debbie had agreed to come at the insistence of her mother who said, "Please, do all you can to save this marriage—for the children's sake."

But neither one of them knew how their marriage could ever work.

"We try to talk," Debbie explained, "but the more we talk, the more frustrated I get. I've tried everything I know how to do. I've prayed, read books, and gone to seminars—but always by myself. Then he looks at me and says, '*We* don't have a problem. *You* have a problem.'"

Then she turned to Bill and said, "You have no idea how much freedom I felt when I finally decided I'd had enough. And now you decide you want this marriage? Oh, I can't do this." She turned her face away to hide the tears.

Shifting his weight, Bill stared down at his hands trying to remember what to do next. He had been coming to counseling alone prior to this session because Debbie refused to come. During that time he learned how to respond to barrages like this. He learned to draw on spiritual resources to maintain inner peace and security, not only in the midst of a conflict but also as a way of life.

Before, when this scenario occurred at home, he usually walked away as she yelled something like, "You always do this to me. You walk out like the gutless wonder you are!"

But things were different now. In the past few weeks Bill had learned some things that had reshaped his whole perspective about himself and his relationship with Debbie.

He learned that along with countless other Christian men and women, he had been taught by churches and seminar leaders in the past that spiritual life results from performing in accordance with certain principles, and that success was determined by outward appearance and behavior. He had not been shown "the internal steps that lead to real empowerment and transformation. He had not been shown how to live."[40]

As he learned about his identity in Christ, he began to feel more peace than he had known in his entire life. He even began to thank God for his marriage crisis, as painful and unsettling as it was. It had brought him to a place of brokenness where he could finally receive God's love and allow God to love Debbie through him.

But right now he prayed for the ability to listen for the heart cry of the tender woman he married, buried somewhere inside this cold, angry person in front of him.

Lord, he prayed, *I know Your presence within me is patient, loving, and kind toward her. So I release myself to You to understand everything she says—even the parts I don't agree with. Thank You that You'll never leave me or forsake me. You're my refuge and my strength, my very life, regardless of what she decides to do.*

Debbie Hit Again

As Debbie sat in her chair, she twisted and looked at Bill, "Why did you marry me?" she asked with eyes flashing. "You behave as if you'd rather be alone most of the time. You're angry. You're harsh with the kids. You don't talk to me. Why did you marry me?"

He could hardly believe what he heard. *Hasn't she seen the changes in me? How could she miss it?* He felt he should respond to her question. But for the moment he had forgotten how to respond.

I (Dallas) prompted him. "Summarize or put in your own words what she said. Don't react, or comment, or answer her question. Just summarize what you heard."

He nodded and said, "You're saying you don't know why I married you in the first place, because I seem to resent you and the kids being around."

"Yes," she said. "You hide in your computer room, and you bury yourself in work."

He summarized, "I'm unavailable to you and the kids."

"Yes," she said, her lips trembling. "And if you think a few sessions of counseling will solve it, you've got another think coming!"

"You want me to know you're hurt and angry and a few counseling sessions will not convince you that things could be different between us. Is that right?"

"Yes," she said, dabbing at tears now running freely down her face.

Moments passed. The only sounds were the ticking of a clock and Debbie blowing her nose.

Bill Listens

He looked at me as if asking for help, and I mouthed the words, "Say more."

"Is there more?" he asked, handing her another tissue.

"Yes," Debbie sobbed. "I don't really want to end our relationship. I never have."

He paused a moment, searching her face. "You don't want out of the marriage," he said.

"I didn't say that," she snapped. "Don't jump to conclusions! I said I didn't want to end the relationship. I'm just so frustrated and tired because nothing ever changes."

Bill repeated, "You're worn out and frustrated because there's no apparent change."

"Yes," she answered. "I've tried everything ... seminars ... books ... telling you how I felt. But you just said I was the one who was unhappy so I needed to go get help."

A frown deepened the lines in his forehead, and his voice became almost a whisper, "I blamed you for everything, and you saw no evidence that I took responsibility for my part of the problem."

"I can't hear you," she said.

He cleared his throat and raised his voice. "I blamed you and I took no part in the responsibility."

"That's it. You got it," she said.

He waited and when she remained silent, he asked, "Anything more?"

When she finally spoke, her voice was softer. "I needed time away to think clearly and pray."

"You were really hurting and you needed time to think things over and talk with the Lord," he said.

"Yes," she said, her eyes filling again as she remembered that difficult time.

He waited. Finally he took a deep breath and said, "Can you say more?"

She shrugged her shoulders. "It seemed like the only solution," she said.

"So," he restated, "at the time you thought getting away was the only constructive choice you had?"

"Right," she said, turning back to him and searching his face. "Anything else?"

She thought for a moment and sighed. "No, I think that's all there is right now."

Bill Decides to Go Deeper

Now was his opportunity to ask questions or make statements about what she said. "May I ask you a question?" he asked.

She nodded.

"You mentioned you were frustrated and angry when you left. I'm wondering what else were you feeling?"

She looked at him a moment and said, "I thought you didn't

care any more and I felt crushed. It was like you were behind a steel door and I couldn't get through."

He reflected, "You felt completely closed out. Alone. And you were deeply hurt."

She nodded her head, with her chin quivering and tears streaming again.

Bill had always been uncomfortable with her tears. He felt so helpless. Was she falling apart? Had he made things worse? Was she manipulating him?

I motioned for him to just wait.

When she reached for another tissue and blew her nose, he nodded and mouthed the words, "Say more."

They continued on as if she was breaking a trail through fresh snow and he followed in her footsteps. With quiet concentration he worked to understand her.

Sometimes he used her exact words and sometimes he paraphrased with his own words. Sometimes he just nodded and said, "uh-huh," to encourage her. Sometimes, when she paused a moment, he invited her to say more. Sometimes he asked her permission to ask an open question, respecting her right to say no.

When their time with us had come to a close that day, Bill had reached a place of understanding he had never before experienced with his wife. He entered a strange new world where winning the argument or protecting himself was not the goal.

But could they stay in this new world? No one stays there 100 percent of the time. But when couples know how to use the gift of listening, they can return to the place of understanding and peace. It's a matter of deciding, *Do I want to go there?*

Bill knew he needed more coaching and experience in order to break old patterns and to maintain the gains he had made. And Debbie was now ready to learn, too.

I handed them a brochure explaining The Gift of Listening seminar, which would teach them discovery listening skills and discovery talking skills anchored in Christ.

Breaking Old Patterns

Part of what happened that day had happened many times in the past.

Debbie would talk and often cry.

And Bill would rarely express his point of view. Usually he got very quiet.

In fact, the more she talked, Bill grew quieter; and as he grew quiet, the more Debbie talked.

This time something different happened. This time he actually listened to what she had to say—and he responded! He summarized the information and listened in such a way that she felt his participation. In the process he not only understood her, he helped her drain off the fear and hurt that had fueled her anger.

But what did Debbie understand about Bill? What about his hidden thoughts and feelings? In her past efforts to understand him, she had assumed a great deal. She had filled in the blanks about how *she thought* he felt about her, through the filter of her own low self-esteem and past experiences with men. How can she possibly know the truth about what he really thinks and feels if he does not tell her?

Bill, on the other hand, often did not know his own "truth." Long ago, he had decided to bury painful emotions because he got into trouble whenever he expressed them. When he buried his feelings, he threw away his joy and tenderness as well. As a result, he felt unable to connect deeply at a heart level with anyone—not with God nor Debbie, not even with himself.

Now he had begun to make a safe place for her to begin trusting him again. But how long can she stay vulnerable and open if he won't allow her into his private world?

Bill's Private World

Bill and Debbie agreed to attend a Gift of Listening seminar. In the sessions, Debbie would also learn about discovery listening and discovery talking anchored in God's grace. And Bill would learn to express his hidden heart.During the seminar, Bill began to open up—but he still risked very little of himself. When the seminar was completed, Debbie turned to face him. "Okay, now we both know how to listen," she said. "But up until now, I've done most of the talking. And even though it's great, I'm beginning to feel 'hung out' like I am the exposed one, but you haven't risked anything." She continued, "I want to hear from you. What are you thinking? What are you feeling?"

"Well," he replied, "as a matter of fact, I'd like to talk about that. I have some thoughts about why I've seemed angry and aloof."

Bill Opens Up

As an engineer, Bill liked having things all figured out before he spoke. But he remembered how I cautioned him about his tendency to cycle everything over and over in his head.

"If you'll invite her to help you think out loud," I had said, "you will be able to sort things out much faster, and you will have the benefit of her summary to clarify things. But most importantly, she will feel loved and included in your life."

Bill cleared his throat. "I hardly know where to begin," he said.

He tried to remember the workshop drawing of the hand with fingers where he worked through an issue as Debbie listened and summarized.

At the time, he felt uncomfortable. But now he was going back through that exercise again and again in his mind, visually reproducing the hand diagram, trying to express to Debbie what he saw and heard, and what he thought, felt, and wanted.

"Would you mind summarizing and just letting me sort out some things?" he asked.

"Sure," she said.

"Well," he began, "I see myself coming in the door from work, grabbing something to drink, and walking straight to my computer room. Maybe I say 'hello' to you and the kids—maybe I don't. But then I remember hearing you say how my actions bothered you."

She summarized. "You remember walking directly to your computer room after work, barely acknowledging the kids and me—and you remember me talking about how this bothered me."

He nodded and mentally moved from the *think* and *feel* fingers to the *want* finger. "At the time, all I wanted was to see if I got any e-mail, to put the day out of my mind, and to get away from people."

She summarized: "So you wanted to get away from everything and lose yourself on your computer," she said.

"Yeah," he said, "I just wanted to numb out, I guess. I didn't want to hurt you and the kids. That wasn't the point at all."

She rephrased, "You had no desire to hurt us. You just wanted to retreat from the world awhile?"

"Yeah, that's it," he said. "I just needed to get away from everything."

"You needed a break?" she said, feeling her growing impatience and reminding herself to take a deep breath and let Jesus do this through her.

"Yes, that's it," he said.

Inside, he thought, *Let's see … where do I go from here?*

Bill Goes Deeper

Mentally, he moved to the *see/hear* finger on the discovery talking hand diagram, and continued, "I hear you say you often see a frown and you *think* I'm tense and upset with you and the girls."

Debbie held her hand up to stop him. Although she didn't want to interrupt his train of thought, she was having trouble concentrating. Her thoughts had already begun to wander to what *she* wanted to say. She knew she had to anchor and possibly hear that phrase again. "Let me see if I've got that part," she said. "You heard me say you look angry when you come home from work … that you have a frown and you look and sound uptight?"

"Yes," he said. "And you think it's about you."

"And the girls and I think you're mad at us," she returned.

"Yes," he said thoughtfully, "and I want you to know that I'm not aware of being mad at you. I'm just stressed."

In his mind, he had just moved to the *feel* finger on the hand.

"You're not mad at us," she said, as she prayed for more patience. "You're just tense from work?"

"Yeah," he sighed.

After a long silence, she asked, "Is there more?"

"I was just thinking about work," he said. "How great it is to have this job ... but the pressure really gets to me."

Bill Expresses How He Feels

"The pressure?" Debbie reflected only the feeling word back to him because she remembered that feelings are the most important part of the message. She also recalled that if you hooked up a speaking person to a biofeedback machine, you could physically observe his tension level go down as he began to share and hear his feelings summarized.

"Yeah," he said—oblivious to what she had discovered. "I feel anxious I guess ... just like any minute someone is going to say, 'You're not the man we thought you were for this job.'"

"You feel uneasy that at any time you might become a victim of downsizing," she summarized.

In his mind, he went back to the *think* finger of the "talking" hand. "I know it sounds crazy," he said, "because I was chosen for the job and I'm doing the work ... but it's like there's a voice inside me saying, 'You're not worth what they pay you. Surely someone else could do it better.'"

Debbie Holds Her Tongue

Desperately, she wanted to interrupt and tell Bill how wrong he was to think this way. He was every bit as good as the others. Everyone thought so. But she remembered how in the past her attempts to talk him out of his feelings had backfired and how she could help him powerfully only by letting him hear himself.

"You think this sounds crazy because you know they chose you and that you're doing the job they've asked you to do—but you tell yourself you're not worthy of what they pay you and someone else could do it better."

"You know," he said, rubbing his chin, "if I were listening to someone else say what I just said, I'd ask him the question, 'Who does that sound like?'"

"May I ask you the question?" she said.

"Just a minute," he said. "I think I'm onto something here ... it sounds to me ... could it be I'm listening to the Accuser—or one of his messengers?"

A New Level of Understanding

"So," she said, "you realize you've been listening to the Enemy tell you how unworthy you are." She thought how incredible that he would come to that realization without her telling him—and immediately she felt convicted. *Lord, forgive me for thinking I must be his Holy Spirit.*

"Man," he mused, "to think that I've been listening to the Deceiver. How did I let him sneak up on me like that?"

She remembered the instruction that as the listener you don't answer questions at a time like this, you only reflect them. "So," she said, "you're asking yourself how you could let this happen."

He sighed, "Maybe, if I'd gotten this out earlier, I would have caught the deception and saved myself a lot of grief."

"You're thinking if we'd had this conversation earlier, you might have detected the lies and spared yourself some pain?" she echoed.

Relieved at the discovery he had made, he laughed at himself. "What a fool I've been," he said, reaching over to hug her.

"You want me to know you've been a fool ..." she said.

Now they were both laughing.

"Thank You, Lord," he prayed. "Thank you for giving my wife ears to hear so I could understand more clearly what You're trying to show me."

"Thank You, Lord, for giving me the grace to listen and let Bill discover what You wanted him to know," she added.

The Scripture drifted through her mind. *"Love is patient, love is kind ... It is not rude, it is not self-seeking, it is not easily angered, it keeps no record of wrongs ... It always protects, always trusts, always hopes, always perseveres (1 Cor. 13:4–7).*

In the next chapter, you will see what to do when understanding is not enough—when you need to add some additional problem-solving skills in order to work together in harmony.

Questions for Personal Reflection or Group Discussion:

- *What's your reaction to the account of Debbie and Bill? What questions, if any, does it generate in your mind? What difference will it make in your life when you apply the principles and skills they used?*

13

When You Need More Problem-Solving Skills

*A good listener tries to understand what the other person
is saying. In the end he may disagree sharply, but
because he disagrees, he wants to know exactly
what it is he is disagreeing with.*
Kenneth A. Wells

Several weeks after the Gift of Listening seminar, Debbie came to see us. As she dropped heavily into a chair, I (Dallas) said, "Tell me what's been happening since we were last together."

"Well, for one thing, the skills aren't working," she said, with a frown.

"Tell me more."

"Frankly I'm really embarrassed to be here after we stood up and told the group at the seminar how well things were going for us."

"Embarrassed?" I asked.

"Yes! Bill is really trying hard. But I can't seem to get with the program," she said staring at the floor. "I'm even getting some of the old feelings of disgust toward him and the desire to leave again. What's wrong with me?" Her eyes searched my face. "I try to stay anchored, but obviously I'm not doing it right."

"Sounds like you feel like you are back to square one," I said.

"Well, yes. I know the skills work because they work for us when we use them. But it just seems like I can't or I won't use them when I really need to. And I start to blame him. It's almost like I want to I hurt him—like he's the enemy or something."

"So you do use the skills sometimes with success, but you want to use them consistently."

She nodded.

"But you feel alarmed and confused that you still want to control him and punish him for not measuring up. Is that right?"

"Right," she affirmed.

In the next few pages, you will learn what to do when discovery listening and talking skills don't seem to work.

Getting Started on the Right Foot

Sometimes difficulty with the skills is simply a "mechanical" problem or a matter of fine-tuning the way you get started.

When you want to have a heavy discussion with someone, here are some tips to help you avoid trouble.

For "Heavy" Issues

Suppose you're having a conflict with someone, or you are concerned you might have a conflict if you don't explain yourself carefully. Here's how to get started on the right foot. It may sound a little businesslike and impersonal, but when you face a heavy issue, these steps can really help to support the relationship.

1. Begin with each person involved agreeing to be open about a *specific* topic you will discuss. Sticking with one issue at a time

helps you avoid getting off the subject and never thoroughly resolving anything. Agreeing to be open means that each person is prepared to speak for himself without hiding important information that needs to be on the table in order for the issue to be resolved.

2. Schedule a starting time—and a length of time you will commit to this process. We recommend short spans of time because heart-to-heart communication demands intense concentration and requires lots of emotional energy. Twenty to thirty minutes is usually plenty of time to begin problem solving. You don't have to solve the problem in one sitting. If you get interrupted or do not finish within the agreed upon length of time, agree to a time to continue. If you merely say, "Let's continue at a *later time*," the later time may never come around.

Conflict Resolution

Sometimes understanding and discovery, using all the skills you have learned so far, isn't enough. There are times when you need another skill—problem solving. Problem solving helps you when you need to make a joint decision but you have different points of view. How do you bring your different points of view together?

For example, what if you are married and you need to decide about how to handle the kids, or you are roommates and you need to determine housekeeping rules, or you are on a search committee for a new pastor and you disagree about which candidates to call? Whatever the issue, there are times when you need to make a joint decision but you disagree.

Don't despair, because you already have 90 percent of the skills you need for problem solving with discovery listening and discovery talking skills.

Problem Solving

1. Anchor

Remember, anchoring is basic to problem solving and to everything in the Christian life. While this section is about changing behavior, we cannot make lasting changes in ourselves. Only the work of the indwelling Christ can change us. Therefore, if you try to fix a problem out of your own intellect and willpower, it won't stay "fixed."

A key to problem solving is to submit your point of view to God, and then by faith invite Him to animate your communication. Are you willing for God to change your point of view if He desires? Can you allow Him to tenderize your heart toward another when you may not agree with his or her viewpoint? If you are willing, then simply proceed, trusting that God is communicating through your mind and your heart. Then just "rest" as you observe Him at work.

2. Reach an Understanding

If you have not already done so, use the talking and listening skills to determine exactly where you disagree. Take as much time as you need here. Understanding each other is crucial to your success in resolving the issue.

Understanding Versus Agreement

There's a huge difference between understanding and agreement. In the early years of our marriage I (Dallas) thought it was important to trade in the old car for a new one every two years. I saw my Dad do that, and I thought that's what a real man does. We were in the ministry after graduating from college, poor as church mice, and somehow Nancy didn't understand my "need" for a new car. I explained all the reasons why it made good sound sense to do this, going over and over it again each time she had an objection.

I thought that agreement was essential in a good marriage; therefore in order to do what I wanted to do, I had to wear her down with my logical, rational arguments.

She would finally agree just to shut me up, even though she knew it was an unwise decision. If we had known how to thoroughly understand the issue at that time, perhaps I would have discovered that I was trying to copy my father, rather than adjust to our meager circumstances. We have discovered that when we use discovery listening skills, with the intention of understanding and not manipulating, we do not need to see eye to eye on every issue. We just need to thoroughly understand our underlying motivations.

When you have reached a clear understanding of your different points of view and have submitted your mind and heart to the will of God, you are ready to brainstorm.

3. Brainstorm

To brainstorm means to generate and record as many solutions as possible without evaluating them.

Bill and Debbie chose the destructive pattern that brought them into counseling—his isolation from the family and her fear of abandonment which caused her to lash out in pain and anger, which caused him to further withdraw, which prompted more fear and anger on her part.

Clearly this was a God-sized job, but they wanted to consciously choose some different behaviors—things they wanted the Holy Spirit to accomplish through them.

Here are some of their brainstorming ideas about how to change their isolating/reacting cycle:

- *"I'd like to make time to just talk about how things are going between us,"* he said, jotting down his idea.
- *"I'd like for us to pray together,"* she said, adding to the list.
- *"I'd also like a regular date night,"* she said.
- *"I'd like a hug after we get in bed, which would mean going to bed at the same time,"* he said, with a wink.
- *"I'd like thirty minutes in the evening with the TV off just being with the girls—reading or playing games or just talking."*

After they completed this list of ideas, they went to the next step: evaluating.

4. Evaluate

Here you simply decide which options you want to eliminate. Then you prioritize the ones you want to work with. Start with just one or two that you both like.

Here's Bill and Debbie's evaluating process:

"I really like your idea about making time to talk. How about combining it with praying together?" she said.

"Okay, I had in mind turning off the television twenty minutes after the kids are in bed and sharing how the day has gone, or whatever else is on our minds."

"That sounds great," she said, checking off those ideas as "keepers."

"It's a deal," he said. "Now I think we'd better stop with these two things and see how we do. But I have another concern. Care to hear about it?"

"Okay," she said.

He cocked his head and smiled at her. "I don't want you to remind me about this agreement because you're afraid I'll forget. That feels like you're parenting me. I helped make this agreement and I have as much at stake as you do in its success. What did you hear me say?"

After she paraphrased, she laughed, her eyes wide with innocence. "Do I do that?"

"You're asking me if you do that," he said, and they both laughed.

All that remained was to set a trial period and a time to evaluate how their plan was working.

5. Trial Period and Reevaluate

"Let's try this for a week," Bill said. "How about next Sunday afternoon at 3 o'clock to see how we're doing?"

"Okay with me," Debbie said.

When they meet in a week, if they think the plan isn't working, they can modify it and/or go back to the above list, choose other behaviors to try, or add other items.

In the next chapter you will learn about a major situation when the skills do not work: bitterness in the relationship.

Action Step

1. Choose an issue with your partner that requires problem solving. Use the hand diagrams to understand the problem from both points of view.

2. Work through the problem-solving steps:
- *Anchor*
- *Understand*
- *Brainstorm*
- *Evaluate and prioritize*
- *Trial period*
- *Reevaluate until you reach a mutually agreeable solution*

Questions for Personal Reflection or Group Discussion

- *What are questions or concerns you may have about what you read in this chapter?*

- *What have you learned from this chapter that could make a difference when you need to reach an agreement with someone?*

14

"The Empty Chair"

*Bear with each other and forgive whatever grievances you may
have against one another. Forgive as the Lord forgave you.*
Colossians 3:13

The gift of listening can be like taking a giant spoon to your
relationship, stirring up the "junk" that needs to surface, as well as
the treasure of your new nature in Christ. God's way to remove the
junk, cleanse your relationship, and give you a fresh start is through
drawing on His grace to forgive. God demonstrated His grace by forgiving you the instant you confessed your need and invited Christ
to take up residence in you. He forgave everything—past, present,
and future. However, for you to find the freedom and peace that
goes with grace, you need to agree with God that you are forgiven.
And then, by His grace, you can pass forgiveness on to others.

Many people tell us, "I know God forgives me, but I can't forgive myself." Oftentimes we respond with, "How can you place

yourself above God?" If you can't forgive yourself, then in effect you are saying, "I'm refusing to receive your grace, God. I reject your gift." Often these same people wouldn't think of refusing to forgive another person. Their bitterness toward another is sin. However they do not see that bitterness toward the self, someone whom God loves, is likewise sinful.

In your anger do not sin. Do not let the sun go down while you are still angry, and do not give the devil a foothold (Eph. 4:26–27).

What if you have allowed the sun to go down many times on your anger either toward yourself or someone else? What if bitterness now has strong, deep roots in your heart?

That's what happened to Kim. Remember her from the first chapter? As she was planning her husband's fortieth birthday party, Kim found evidence of her husband's affair with her best friend.

Here's what happened when Kim came in for her first counseling session. She had already learned about a fresh, new, personal understanding of God's grace. Yet with good reason, she was still furious and humiliated from Don's betrayal.

If someone has betrayed you, you've lost a relationship, experienced the death of someone close, or suffered any other event that leaves you bitter, you can find peace as you apply the principles in this chapter.

Or perhaps as you give the gift of listening, you find someone else who needs to forgive. You can take the listener's role in this chapter by giving the gift of listening and applying God's grace to the situation.

Kim huddled in the corner of the couch in my (Nancy's) office, sobbing out the story of Don's betrayal. "Nothing will ever be the same again," she said, as she wrapped her arms around herself and rocked as if comforting a small child.

After she had poured out her grief and used up most of a box of tissues, I placed a chair in front of her and asked her to imagine Don sitting in the chair.

"What does he look like?" I asked.

"You know," she said, looking up through her tears and frowning.

"Yes," I said, "but I want you to see Don in your mind's eye as if he's sitting there."

"Okay," she said, humoring me. "He's tall. And he has dark gray eyes. Is that what you mean?"

"He'd be slouched," she continued. "You'd have to move the chair back because his legs would be clear out to here." She indicated a place tight against her knees.

I moved the chair back.

"Now describe to him what he's done to you," I said. "Speak to him directly as if he's actually here. Say things you have already said or things you haven't said but feel strongly such as 'Don, you have hurt me deeply,'" I prompted.

She stared at the empty chair a few moments collecting her thoughts. Then she said,

"You have hurt me deeply. You betrayed me. You have ruined our lives. And the worst part is ... there is no way I could ever trust you again. I hate you, Don."

She reached for a tissue and dabbed at the tears.

"I hate you! I hate you!" she said, pounding her fists on her lap. "I trusted you completely. Everyone did. No one would ever have dreamed you could do this. And with Claudia! Why did you have to choose my best friend? All at once, I've lost you and my best friend. Who do I have to go to now? I hate you. I hate you!" she cried, as she hugged herself and rocked again.

After a few seconds, she continued. "I thought as a Christian you were committed forever like I was. And where is God in all this?" Looking upward, she cried out, "God, I trusted You. I feel like I've lost You, too!" The wailing grew louder as she doubled over, knees pulled up, rounding herself into a ball.

"It feels like everyone has deserted you," I summarized. "Even God seems far away."

"Yes," she said nodding and rocking and sobbing. "Yes."

After a few minutes the crying subsided and I asked, "Is there more?"

She sat up and blew her nose. "No," she said, leaning back and looking at me through red eyes. After a moment, she said, "You know, the funny thing is I didn't realize I felt that way—about God I mean. But it's true. I haven't been able to pray since all this happened. It seems like all I do is cry."

"Tell it to Don," I said, pointing her back to the chair.

"Because of you, my whole life is on hold. In fact, I can't even imagine the future," she said to the chair.

"There doesn't appear to be a future," I said.

"Well, not exactly," she said, looking at me. "God is not dead. I know He's there and I'll find Him—no thanks to you, Don," she said, glaring at the chair.

"So you know that God is there and that you will once more experience His presence."

"Yes," she said.

"Kim, would you be willing to put God in the chair instead of Don for a moment?"

"Okay," she said, as she wrinkled her brow at me and smiled faintly. "You're the counselor. Whatever you say."

"Would you just tell the Lord what you're thinking and feeling about Him?"

"Sure," she said, looking at the chair. "Lord, I prayed for a Christian husband for so long and even wrote down the godly characteristics I wanted. I trusted You. And when I met Don, I knew he was the one You gave me. And it wasn't just me. Mom and Dad—everyone—agreed. Don was the one."

After a pause, she continued. "What happened, God? I don't understand. Life was so good. Perfect, really. Yes, well, Don now says life wasn't perfect. He admits he felt I took him for granted and that he's felt like I insisted on having life on my own terms ... that he's felt controlled and that he's been on a leash for some time."

"You prayed for Don and God delivered him. You knew that. But Don now admits he's felt restrained for some time now."

"Yes, she agreed, "but what's with that? He could have told me. We could have talked things out. He didn't have to blow up our lives because he felt stifled."

"You want God to know that Don's behavior was way out of proportion to your crime."

"Yes," she said.

For most of the hour, we continued with her talking to the chair and to me, as I used discovery listening to help her express herself. Eventually, I said to her, "Kim, could I ask you a question?"

When she nodded, I said, "Would you like to begin the process of clearing the deck of all this? Getting a clean start so that you can get past this?"

"Of course," she said. "That's why I came to you."

"Based on the fact that you are one with Christ and that His nature is now at your disposal to deal with this, would you be willing to release Don to Christ and stop the torment you're experiencing? You've said you're not sleeping or eating, and you can't stop cycling your anger and grief. Right?"

"Right," she said.

"Would you be willing to forgive by faith? That is, trust Christ in you to do the forgiving in you and through you?"

"Yes, as long as you don't expect me to feel like it."

"Fine," I said. "All the Holy Spirit needs is your willingness to forgive. And remember, it's a process. Along with bitterness comes a whole host of thoughts you need to take captive. But until you forgive as an act of obedience, you give Satan the opportunity to torment you with captivating thoughts that stubbornly refuse to go away."

"I can sure identify with the tormenting part," she said.

"Okay," I said, "put Don back in the chair, and go down your list of grievances. Begin each statement with the phrase, 'In the name of Jesus, I forgive you for ...' and tell him one by one how he's hurt you."

"In the name of Jesus, I forgive you for betraying me with Claudia," she said.

"I forgive you for causing so much anger and confusion in the kids."

"I forgive you for blowing your 'great guy' image forever."

"I forgive you for destroying my trust and my life ... for making me question everything, even God's love."

She paused and after a moment. I asked, "Is there more?"

"For opening us up to the Destroyer—to all this hatred."

After another pause, I asked, "Anything more?"

"No," she said. "That's it for now."

"More things may come to mind later," I said, "and you can return Don to this empty chair and continue this process. But let's go on to the next step. This part's the hardest for many people. Will you ask Don to forgive you?"

Seeing the startled look on her face, I added, "Whenever we've been victimized by someone, we usually respond in sinful ways like hatred and rage toward that person."

"Okay, I get the point," she said. "Don, I have hated you. I have even wished you dead." She looked down at her hands folding and refolding a damp tissue. "I ask you to forgive me for that and for the ways I've controlled you, although you could have chosen a different way to tell me. Still, I was wrong to take you for granted and to run over you at times. Forgive me for that."

She paused to think some more. Then she added, "Don, forgive me for all the screaming I've done and the hateful things I've said to you. I see how sad you are and I realize I've been glad you are suffering. Forgive me for not wanting to ever forgive you—for wanting you to suffer the rest of your life."

Now she was crying again, only this time in remorse.

After a moment, I asked her, "Would you be willing to pray for Don?"

"Yes," she said, without hesitation. "Lord, I pray for Don. He's done a terrible thing and he's suffering for it. I do pray that he finds peace and comfort in You. I know there's nothing You don't forgive, and I pray that this forgiveness becomes real for Don and for everyone concerned, even Claudia."

Kim had come full circle. She had found the love of Christ for Don that resided within her. She had loosened the hold of dark, tormenting thoughts, and now she was ready for another step.

"Would you be willing to put yourself, the self who has been so angry, in the chair?" I said.

"Sure," she said. "What for?"

"Just as Don needed your forgiveness, you need it as well."

"Okay," she said. "Here goes."

"What do you feel toward her?" I asked, pointing to chair.

"She's been pretty wrapped up in herself, I'd say," she said, with a laugh.

"Tell her," I said, pointing to the chair.

"You got totally off balance there, girl. Did you forget that Christ has forgiven you everything? Agreeably this is a toughie to put behind you, but you weren't ever promised a trouble-free life. Jesus has not forsaken you. It's time to draw on His presence, and to stop wallowing in self-pity. I forgive you."

She paused a moment and then she said, "By the way, your life isn't over. It will be different, but not over. Your kids are watching you to see how you handle this. You have been hurt and you have reacted by hurting everyone around you. I don't approve of what you've done, but I do forgive you, in the name of Jesus."

"Now, Kim, would you pray for her, too?"

She said, "Lord Jesus, let the fountain of living water spring up in her and wash her clean. And yet I know she's already forgiven— at the cross when You paid the price for her sin."

She paused a moment and said softly, a faint smile beginning to lift the corners of her mouth, "Come, Holy Spirit, and fill her with peace."

In order to help her feel together again with the self she was addressing in the empty chair, I said, "Think about the Lord standing with His arms outstretched between you and the self you have just forgiven. Now think about Him embracing you and the other Kim, pulling both of you into each other and into Himself."

"... *just as you are in me and I am in you. May they also be in us*" (John 17:21).

"And, as your sister in Christ, I forgive you, too," I said, remembering the passage about forgiving a broken brother or sister in the Lord.

"You ought to forgive and comfort him, so that he will not be overwhelmed by excessive sorrow ..." (2 Cor. 2:7).

She wept tears of relief.

Before we finished, we put Claudia into the chair and she went through her list of grievances against her and forgave her for each one. Then she prayed for her, as well.

After we finished, she said to me, calmly, "Oh, the peace that passes understanding. I can feel it once again."

Shortly after this intense session, Kim and Don began their reconciliation. And the rest is history.

If bitterness torments you, use the empty chair exercise to help you experience the peace that Kim found that day. You may not cover everything at one time as we did in this chapter, but this is a way to restore God's peace in your life.

Action Step 1

Think of someone you're having trouble forgiving—and put this person in the empty chair. The person may be you, or perhaps you are angry with God.

Go down your mental list of grievances against the person and tell him how he's angered, saddened, or frightened you.

Tell him what his behavior has cost you, as far as you can determine. For example, "Because of you I've never trusted men. But I keep choosing men just like you."

After you have drained off all the feelings and there seems nothing more to say, go down your list of grievances and extend forgiveness in Jesus' name for each one: In the name of Jesus I forgive you for ...

Then ask the person in the empty chair to forgive you. Go down your list. (Whenever we've been hurt, we usually have sinful responses—hatred, bitterness, and vengeful thoughts, wanting bad things to happen to them, etc.) Forgive me for ...

Now take this person to the cross of Christ and release him or her to Him.

Pray a blessing on them. Lord, I turn over _____ to you. I pray _____ will find peace, salvation (or whatever the needs may be).

Action Step 2

After you've forgiven someone, and you know you have offended and/or wounded him, work through this exercise alone and then prayerfully consider going to that person. Use discovery listening to listen to his responses.

1. Specify what you did or didn't do for which you are asking forgiveness.

2. State "I was wrong. Will you forgive me?"

3. Give a specific example. For example, "When you were young I was too busy to give you the love or attention you needed and deserved from me."

4. Tell him how you think it must have made him feel: "It must have hurt you deeply."

15

Coming Full Circle

*You and I never outgrow our need to communicate what
it feels like in our separate, private worlds of experience.
Unfortunately there is no similar need to be the one who
listens. Listening isn't a need you have, it's gift you give.*
Michael Nichols[41]

As we bring this book to a close, we end with a story from
someone who now experiences the gift of listening on a regular basis.

Pastor Fred told us about counseling a couple who were in their
early sixties. Harold and Mildred accumulated years of tremendous
pain and woundedness in relationships, so they had spent years in
recovery groups and therapy. Finally in a move of desperation, the
couple made an appointment with Pastor Fred.

He told us, "This couple arrived late for their appointment, then
announced they needed to leave early. Harold said, 'I'm so sorry. We
only have thirty minutes.'"

The pastor said, "Without the gift of listening, in the past I would have told the couple, 'Forget it. I don't have enough time to say what you need to hear. It's going to take a lot longer than thirty minutes.' Because of my newfound listening ability in Christ, I wasn't worried about the lack of time so I said, 'You guys are sixty years old and have sixty years' worth of junk, so I have no expectation of figuring it out. If you're coming for any suggestion from me as to what to do next, it's not going to happen. But I've got good news for you. Jesus, who has been with you every second of your sixty years, knows exactly all the stuff that's tangled you up and hurt you. Jesus is here and I'm going to ask Him if He'll just make Himself known in your spirits so that this junk can get straightened out. I admit that I don't have a clue. I'm only going to facilitate and keep listening as you tell your story, and see if Jesus will birth some healing.'"

As Harold and Mildred began to talk, Pastor Fred facilitated their communication with each other. He'd asked, "What did you hear Mildred say?" or "Okay, let Mildred tell you what she heard you say." Then Harold would summarize. And Pastor Fred would turn to Mildred and say, "Okay, now slow down and make sure you understand what Harold's saying. And suddenly came the long pause. Harold and Mildred looked at each other and Harold said, "I just never thought of it that way before."

Pastor Fred recognized the "discovery" or the breakthrough he had prayed for and he said to them, "I just want you to hold your wife's hand and say that again, and I want you to listen." Then he asked the couple to thank the Lord for what just happened.

In about thirty minutes, Harold and Mildred had dealt with the issue that brought them into counseling that day because they made discoveries through listening. Pastor Fred and the couple thanked the Lord and they prepared to leave. As they turned to walk out the office door, Harold said, "My gosh, I've been in therapy for over twenty years and I never had this kind of result before."

Pastor Fred and others like him are discovering that Jesus, the Wonderful Counselor and the Great Physician, can untangle any relationship. God has the fixing and the healing ability so the burden upon the helping person is lifted. We don't have to fix each other. Instead we are set free to listen to one another, then be openly transparent with one another and let God do the fixing.

When we listen to one another, there is a mutual sharing and clarification of the burden. In a sense there is a sharing of the burden. And often the listener will discover a solution during the listening process. But many problems are long term and very complex. Someone has said the reason we are called sheep in the Bible is because sheep have little short legs and were never intended to carry heavy burdens. Jesus wants us to "rest" while He carries the burdens. He is the Shepherd. He is the Wonderful Counselor.

Many are worn out from "helping." Not just pastors, but small group leaders, friends, parents, spouses—anyone who has listening ears but who feels responsible to solve problems.

People have a great hunger to be heard, but you will soon burn out if you think you have to "fix" the problems they bring to you. Remember that the Wonderful Counselor is in you and in every believer.

You can "rest" the problems with Jesus. He is the burden bearer. He is the Wonderful Counselor. He's the One who took this problem on Himself when He died. He's the One who will carry the responsibility for solving the problem, if you let Him.

The act of laying the burden at the foot of the cross can be as simple as a prayer.

"Lord, thank You that You are the Wonderful Counselor. Thank You for taking the burden; we (I) release it to You. Thank You for the wisdom, love, everything we need as we release this issue into Your care."

Having read this far, you have probably been reminded of some things you already knew about listening, but perhaps you came to realize that careful, intentional listening is even more important and difficult than you realized. The desire to be in the spotlight is so compelling that even when we do listen, it's not with the intent to understand, but to form a rebuttal or a reply when it's our turn to talk. Truly listening is an expression of the nature of God within us, contrary to our natural, unspiritual inclinations apart from Christ.

Because we've witnessed the truth of this work of God in the lives of the many people in our counseling offices, we long to see the gift of listening spread until it floods our homes, our churches, our businesses, and is evident virtually any place where Christians gather to communicate or to interface with the world.

In the bigger picture, giving the gift of listening as an expression of God's indwelling presence not only transforms your personal and professional relationships, but it can also help bring understanding and healing across the racial divide, and between the diverse and varied parts of the body of Christ. We long to see an army of believers committed to extending a hearing heart and an understanding mind to one another and to a hurting world. You provide the unique personality and the packaging through which the life of God moves. Through His grace, He provides everything else.

We've laid out a trail of Scripture and information God has brought across our path with a prayer that you will journey far beyond what you learned here. We would love to hear your stories about what God is doing as you apply the gift of listening or about how we can be of further assistance along your way. You can reach us at **www.canyouhearmenow.org** or email **dallas@bridgingministries.org** or **nancy@bridgingministries.org**.

appendix a

Anchoring Bibliography

Campbell, Ross. *How to Really Love Your Child*. Colorado Springs, Colo.: Cook Communications Ministries, 1977, 1992.

Edwards, Gene. *Secret to the Christian Life*. Wheaton, Ill.: Tyndale House Publishers, Inc., 1991.

Ferguson, David and Teresa. *Never Alone*. Wheaton, Ill.: Tyndale House Publishers, Inc., 2001

Gillham, Anabel. *Confident Woman*. Eugene, Ore.: Harvest House Publishers, 1993.

Gillham, Bill. *Lifetime Guarantee*. Eugene, Ore.: Harvest House Publishers, 1993.

Gillham, Bill. *What God Wishes Christians Knew About Christianity*. Eugene, Ore.: Harvest House Publishers, 1998.

McVey, Steve. *A Divine Invitation*. Eugene, Ore.: Harvest House
Publishers, 2002.

McVey, Steve. *Grace Walk*. Eugene, Ore.: Harvest House
Publishers, 1995.

McVey, Steve. *Grace Rules*. Eugene, Ore.: Harvest House
Publishers, 1998.

McVey, Steve. *Grace Land*. Eugene, Ore.: Harvest House Publishers,
2000.

Nee, Watchman. *The Normal Christian Life*. First published by
Gospel Literature Service, Bombay, India, in 1957; American
edition published by Tyndale House Publishers, Inc., Wheaton,
Ill., in 1977

Needham, David. *Birthright*. Portland, Ore.: Multnomah Press,
1979.

Thomas, W. Ian. *The Saving Life of Christ*. Grand Rapids, Mich.:
Zondervan Publishing House, 1988.

VanVonderen, Jeff. *Families Where Grace Is in Place*. Minneapolis,
Minn.: Bethany House Publishers, 1992.

endnotes

Chapter 2
1. Michael P. Nichols, *The Lost Art of Listening* (New York: Guilford Press, 1955).
2. David Seamands, *Healing of Memories* (Elgin, Ill.: David C. Cook Publishing, 1985).

Chapter 3
3. David Seamands, *Healing Grace* (Indianapolis, Ind.: Light and Life Communications, 1999), 11.
4. Gary Kinnaman, sermon titled "Making Sense of the Christian Faith," Word of Grace Church, Mesa, AZ, June 2, 2002.
5. David and Teresa Ferguson, *Never Alone* (Wheaton, Ill.: Tyndale House Publishers, Inc., 2001), 55.
6. Ibid., 70,71.

Chapter 4
7. Michael P. Nichols, *The Lost Art of Listening* (New York: Guilford Press, 1955), 80.
8. Ibid., 23.
9. Ibid., 25.
10. Ibid., 30.
11. Madelyn Burley-Allen, *Listening: the Forgotten Skill* (New York: John Wiley and Sons, Inc., 1995), 28.
12. Ibid.
13. Adapted from Stephan B. Karkpman's article, "Fairy Tales and Script Drama

Analysis," *Transactional Analysis Bulletin*, No. 26, April 1968, 39–43.

14. Ibid.

Chapter 5

15. Watchman Nee, *The Normal Christian Life* (Wheaton, Ill.: Tyndale House Publishers, Inc., 1977), 141.

16. Steve Farrar, *Anchor Man* (Nashville, Tenn.: Thomas Nelson Publishers, 1998), 3.

17. Oswald Chambers, *My Utmost for His Highest* (1935; reprint, Grand Rapids, MI: Discovery House Publishers, 1992), October 31, "The Trial of Faith."

18. Anabel Gillham, *Confident Woman* (Eugene, Ore.: Harvest House Publishers, 1993), 18.

Chapter 6

19. Michael Nichols, *The Lost Art of Listening* (New York, London: Guilford Press, 1955), 100.

20. Back in the mid-1970s we received leadership training in the Minnesota Couples Communication Program developed by Sherod Miller, Elam Nunnally, and Daniel Wackman at the University of Minnesota. They evolved their work into the highly successful, widely researched program known today as Couples Communication Program, teaching well over 750,000 couples worldwide. We collaborated with them in writing the manual, *Working Together—Improving Communication on the Job*, which applied the same communication skills to the workplace. Through the years we developed our own application and interpretation of their frameworks as they apply to Christians. But we wish to acknowledge their influence on the skill base for the gift of listening.

21. Madelyn Burley-Allen, *Listening, the Forgotten Skill*, (New York: John Wiley & Sons, Inc., 1995), 64.

22. Ross Campbell, M.D. *How to Really Love Your Child* (Colorado Springs, Colo.: Victor Publishing, a Division of Cook Publications, 1936), 47–56.

23. Michael Nichols, *The Lost Art of Listening* (New York, London: Guilford Press, 1955), 154.

24. Ibid.

25. Madelyn Burley-Allen, *Listening, the Forgotten Skill* (New York: John Wiley and Sons, Inc., 1995), 65.

Chapter 7

26. Listening Web site **http://www.listen.org/quotations/quotes.html**

Chapter 8

27. A.W. Tozer, *The Best of Tozer* (Grand Rapids: Baker Book House, 1978), 120.
28. David Ferguson, *Great Commandment Living Conference*, Phoenix, Arizona, February 8–9, 2002.
29. Henry Blackaby and Claude King, *Experiencing God* (Nashville, Tenn.: Lifeway Press, 1990), 43
30. Gene Edwards, *The Secret to the Christian Life* (Wheaton, Ill.: Tyndale House Publishers, Inc., 1991).
31. Ibid.

Chapter 9

32. Michael P. Nichols, *The Lost Art of Listening* (New York: Guilford Press, 1955), 145.
33. Minnesota Couples Communication Program developed by Sherod Miller, Elam Nunnally, and Daniel Wackman, which is now known as Interpersonal Communication Skills Incorporated, 7201 South Broadway, Littleton, Colorado 80122. Discovery talking skills spring from their framework called the Awareness Wheel.

Chapter 10

34. Leonard Sweet, *Post Modern Pilgrims* (Loveland, Colo.: Group Publishing, 1999), 100.
35. David Burns, *The Feeling Good Handbook* (New York: Penguin Putnam, Inc., 1990).
36. Sweet, ibid.
37. Sweet, ibid.
38. Anabel Gillham, *Confident Woman* (Eugene, Ore.: Harvest House Publishers, 1993), 68.

Chapter 12

39. Michael P. Nichols, *The Lost Art of Listening* (New York: The Guilford Press, 1955), 135.
40. Jeff VanVonderen, *Families Where Grace Is in Place* (Minneapolis: Bethany House Publishers, 1992), 45.

Chapter 15

41. Michael P. Nichols, *The Lost Art of Listening* (New York: The Guilford Press, 1955), 251.